Explorations
of the Linguistic
Attitudes
of Teachers

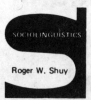

SERIES IN SOCIOLINGUISTICS

Roger W. Shuy, *Series Editor*
Georgetown University and
Center for Applied Linguistics

The term *sociolinguistics* has been used since approximately the mid-1960s to designate the complex intersection of the fields of language and society. Sociologists have used linguistic data, often referring to the expression, *the sociology of language,* to describe and explain social behavior. Linguists, on the other hand, have tended to make use of social behavior to interpret linguistic variation. Still others have conceived of sociolinguistics in a more practical or applied sense, usually related to social dialects in an educational setting or language teaching. These three perspectives, sociological, linguistic and educational, are all legitimate, for it would be difficult to claim that any one group has an exclusive right to the term. It has become apparent increasingly that those who are interested in the ethnography of speaking, language planning, linguistic variation, the dynamics of language change, language attitudes, pragmatics, multi-lingualism and applied sociolinguistics are all concerned with sociolinguistics in one sense or another. As might be expected in any field, some scholars prefer the more linguistically dominating aspects, some the social or ethnographic, and some the applied or relational. Thus sociolinguistics may be studied in a number of different contexts.

This new series of books will cover a broad spectrum of topics which bear on important and changing issues in language and in society. The significance of social, linguistic, and psychological factors as they relate to the understanding of human speech and writing will be emphasized. In the past most language analyses have not taken these factors into account. The most exciting development of recent linguistic theory and research has been the recognition of the roles of context, variability, the continuum, and cross-disciplinary understanding.

explorations
of the linguistic
attitudes of teachers

FREDERICK WILLIAMS

and Associates

Nancy Hewett

Robert Hopper

Leslie M. Miller

Rita C. Naremore

Jack L. Whitehead

NEWBURY HOUSE PUBLISHERS INC., ROWLEY, MASSACHUSETTS

Library of Congress Cataloging in Publication Data

Williams, Frederick, 1933-
    Explorations of the linguistic attitudes of
teachers.

    (Series in sociolinguistics)
    Bibliography: p.
    Includes index.
    1. Sociolinguistics. 2. Teachers–Language.
3. English language in the United States.
I. Hewett, Nancy. II. Title.
P40.W5   301.2'1   76-1890
ISBN 0-88377-052-0

Series cover design by Lois Jefferson Kordaszewski

 NEWBURY HOUSE PUBLISHERS, Inc.

Language Science
Language Teaching
Language Learning

68 Middle Road, Rowley, Massachusetts 01969

Printed in the U.S.A.   First printing: November 1976
                                     5 4 3 2 1

foreword

The study of language attitudes grows out of a number of different academic homes. Involved in the fields of linguistics, psychology, speech and anthropology are the study of human reactions to language, especially as they are related to values, beliefs and attitudes. A pioneer in research of this type is Frederick Williams. In this volume, Williams brings together the recent work which he has carried out with his colleagues in several studies. The focus, in this case, is on the attitude of teachers. It is altogether fitting that a sociolinguistics series include the study of language attitudes, for variability in reaction to language is a rich source of linguistic and cultural insight. The work represented here is particularly timely as it deals with a critical yet relatively uncharted area of study: how teachers make judgments about children on the basis of the child's use of language. Especially important are the sections on stereotyping and cross-cultural judgments, with a focus on Mexican-Americans, Blacks and Anglos. In our recent concern for educational equality in America we have not often looked to language as the cue to such perception and judgment. Although unfair reactions to language use may strike anyone, the problems of minorities are usually exacerbated by such judgments. This book, therefore, represents a significant advance both as a model for research in this field and as an example of how sociolinguistic research can have almost immediate pay-off for practical application to current educational and social concerns.

Roger W. Shuy

Georgetown University and
Center for Applied Lingustics
November 1975

preface

This monograph represents a collection of reports on research into various aspects of linguistic attitudes, particularly attitudes that teachers may hold toward children of different ethnic and social status groups. The first project, the Chicago study of teachers' attitudes, was initiated by the senior author while on the research staff of the Institute for Research on Poverty at the University of Wisconsin during the years 1967-69. Serving at the time as a research branch of the Office of Economic Opportunity, the Institute provided a stimulating intellectual environment and an adequate amount of financial support for the development of studies in contemporary social problem areas.

As many people can easily recall, educational intervention programs were an important part of the War on Poverty, and the language varieties of various target populations in these activities received considerable attention. The attitude research grew out of projects where the main effort was analysis of some of the characteristics of such language variations, particularly with an eye toward problems of educational intervention programs. It became readily apparent, however, that just as important as the existence of linguistic variations were the attitudes held by persons toward these variations. In particular, there was much evidence to suggest that linguistic attitudes play a significant role in the kinds of intervention strategies and practices developed by educational planners.

At the time we were considering such problems, Wallace Lambert, Richard Tucker, and their colleagues at McGill University had already gained substantial insights into this research area. Their cooperation in sharing current research findings with us was an impetus in launching the present series of studies. Also influential in the initiation of these studies was Roger Shuy, who at the time was completing the Detroit dialect project, and who generously shared materials from this project for use as stimulus materials.

In the fall of 1969, the senior researcher moved to The University of Texas where the state itself provided a rich research environment for investigating language variations and attitudes. A grant awarded under the program of the Committee for Basic Research in Education (Grant OEG-0-70-2868 (508)) provided the main financial support for the Texas projects, which constitute almost three-fourths of the activities reported in this monograph. Work in Texas was further facilitated by the enthusiastic cooperation of Jack L. Whitehead in many phases of research planning and implementation.

It was, of course, necessary to gain access to teacher populations in the state of Texas, and we are particularly indebted to Mrs. Mary Galvin of the Texas Education Agency who opened many doors for us. Also, in retrospect, the research commitments of The University of Texas, its School of Communication, and the Center for Communication Research were contributions in a very fundamental way to the maintenance of our activities.

For her assistance in the processes of developing this monograph, a significant share of appreciation must go to Nancy Hewett. While a student at the University of Michigan, Ms. Hewett was working independently in the area of linguistic attitudes and followed our research program with probably a more objective eye than most of us who were in the midst of the research activities. Subsequently, when she moved to The University of Texas and joined our research team, we found her to be one of our best critics. Accordingly, she served very effectively in helping us to prepare the present report for publication. Finally, acknowledgments must go to Markham Publishers and those professional associations who have allowed us to reprint major sections of our reports in the pages of this monograph. Their journals include *The American Educational Research Journal, Speech Monographs, Journal of Speech and Hearing Research, The Central State Speech Journal, Southern Speech,* and *Western Speech.*

Frederick Williams
Los Angeles, California

contents

Explorations of the Linguistic Attitudes of Teachers

chapter 1

LINGUISTIC AND PSYCHOLOGICAL DIMENSIONS
OF THE PROBLEM

Aims

Our everyday experiences, not to mention such literature as Shaw's *Pygmalion,* provide us with an abundance of anecdotal evidence about language and attitude. In an earlier publication, (Williams, 1970a, p. 381), we characterized the relation between language and attitude as follows:

> That our speech, by offering a rich variety of social and ethnic correlates, each of which has attitude correlates in our own and our listeners' behaviors, is one means by which we remind ourselves of social and ethnic boundaries, and is thus a part of the process of social maintenance (or change).

For almost two decades we have had the benefit of an increasing amount of research into the nature of language attitudes. Taken together, this research is beginning to reveal to us those features of language which tend to have a social significance, as well as a definition of such significance in terms of the psychology of human attitudes. In a methodological sense, this research has often represented a productive combination of contemporary strategies for linguistic study with techniques from the psychological study of social consciousness. Most of this research is found on the pages of many different scholarly journals, ranging across linguistics, education, speech communication, and social psychology. However, there seems to be some consensus that the study of linguistic attitudes is a component of the emerging field of sociolinguistics. Much of the research which one can find under the heading of sociolinguistics involves the study of the relationship between variations and the particular features of language and social variables of speakers and speech situations. The topic of linguistic attitudes enters this picture when we consider

1

how individuals, as a part of their range of social knowledge, internalize associations between particular characteristics of language and the people who speak that language. Or put into simple terms, the relationship between linguistic and social variables exists in our "heads" just as it exists as a focus of real world observations. Because, at the heart of the matter, the study of linguistic attitudes focuses upon relations between language and social variables, it is inherently a part of sociolinguistic study. In the largest perspective the aim of this monograph is to integrate a series of research reports into a sociolinguistically oriented framework. By so doing we hope to advance ideas of theory and method on the topic of linguistic attitudes. A secondary aim of the volume is to provide an overall summary of our research on teacher attitudes conducted in the past five years.

Prior to describing any further details, it will be useful to consider a number of the basic assumptions concerning language, language attitudes, and the overall process of how the two interrelate in behavior.

Background to the Problem

Although popular or lay notions of language suggest that there is one right way to speak or write, the linguist sees the systematic nature of all language and does not view any particular variety or dialect as being "superior" or better able to express logical relationships than any other. Thus, the concepts of social as well as regional dialects have emerged as foci for study in their own right.

Sociolinguists use the term "standard dialect" to refer to the dialect which historical accident has codified with formal grammars and dictionaries. It is usually the dialect used by educated writers and speakers and taught in the schools. In the United States the standard dialect is that variety of the language which one hears mostly spoken by announcers or newscasters on the television and radio; consequently it is sometimes called "network" or "broadcast" English.

The linguist, on the other hand, has a homogeneous model for language. He has found it useful in describing language to assume that all speakers of the same dialect have the same generative rules in their heads. The linguist has called those rules, or the abstract set of principles that compose the structure of a language, *competence.* However, what a speaker does with language (i.e., competence) is called *performance.* In other words, competence refers to the nature of language and performance refers to language behavior, both in terms of production and comprehension.

The linguist's homogeneous model is not sufficient for sociolinguists who wish to know about the "interactional" aspects of speech and discourse. They have observed that speakers of a particular dialect will share to *varying degrees* in *varying situations* the features described by the linguist as the model for the dialect in question. To go beyond a homogeneous mode requires consideration of such concepts as performance repertoire, of changing speech styles to suit the occasion, of recognizing the dynamics of culture interacting with language, to name a few.

Sociolinguistic Variables

During the 1960s there were several major efforts untertaken in the United States to study relations between language variation and social stratification. Here social stratification refers to the combined difference in income, occupation, and social class of people. Investigations such as those by William Labov (1966) in New York City and by Roger Shuy and his colleagues (Shuy, Wolfram, and Riley, 1967) in Detroit represented a working combination of sociologic and linguistic research methods (cf. Chapter 2 for more details). These studies introduced the formal incorporation of several components in sociolinguistic study.

Most of these components center around the behavioral sciences' concept of the *variable*. Usually we think of a variable as any phenomenon susceptible to identification, and in behavioral sciences' research further susceptible to manipulation and measurement. In a lay sense, variables constitute the ingredients of a study. Thus, for example, in a sociolinguistic setting one can consider various speech phenomena as linguistic variables, their users as a speaker variable, the setting and usages as situational variables, and even such further items as style, topic, types of listeners, and the like as all variables in their own right. In essence, the variables provide for the definitions of the components of performance situations, and it is the description of such situations and the generality of this description that constitute one of the major thrusts of sociolinguistics. The linguistic features researched in urban language studies have chiefly been those thought correlated with social stratification—for example, the pronunciation of /r/ in New York City or the use of grammatical nonstandard-izations such as multiple negation ("I haven't got none.") in Detroit. These features constitute *linguistic variables* in sociolinguistic study. The range of variation (e.g., different usages, pronunciations) of such variables has been defined as the *linguistic continuum*. Speakers in these studies have been classified in terms of such social variables as education, occupation, and income, as well as sex and age.

In contrast to traditional linguistic field study, the urban language studies have incorporated a quantitative dimension. Whereas the linguist often works with one or only a few informants, the urban researchers have attempted to study groups of speakers so selected as to be representative of a speaker population. That is, they have used the *sampling* methods of sociologic studies. This allows the researcher to use a sample of people in order to make inferences about a population. The consistency with which a variable is found in a specified form in the behavior of a sample of persons gives a basis for making inferences about the population represented by that sample. This basis allows for the use of inferential statistics, providing researchers with a mathematical index for gauging the confidence with which they can make inferences about a linguistic variable in a well-defined population. (For example, inferences can be made about the way persons living on the lower East side of Manhattan pronounce /r/, etc.)

Another aspect of quantification has been in studying the frequency with which variations in a linguistic variable are found, as, for example, the relative frequency with which /r/ is pronounced in particular ways, depending upon the speaker and his situation of speaking. Such quantification is in contrast to the descriptive linguist's usual interest in only the qualitative description of a language. In qualitative description, the linguist attempts to abstract from his observations of speech events the most thorough yet simplest description of the language, as in finding the one set of phonemes that could account for the basic sounds of that language.

Variation which cannot be predicted upon linguistic grounds (as in morphological or phonological conditioning) has traditionally been left undescribed and considered as *free* or *random* variation. By contrast, sociolinguistic researchers have observed that frequencies of this latter type of variation can often be predicted upon the basis of such variables as the speaker's social status and the formality of the speech situation. We would probably find, for example, that a standard-English-speaking person's full articulation of an "-ing" [ŋ] ending would occur 90 to 100 percent of the time in formal speech situations (e.g., as in job interviews). By contrast, something less than this percentage will occur in informal situations (casual, conversational speech) where the incidence of an "in" [-n] allophone typically increases. Here the linguistic variable is the /ŋ/ phoneme; the continuum, the relative incidence of [n] as against [ŋ] realizations; and the situation mainly a differentiation among informal to formal circumstances of speaking.

Urban language research has involved the linguistic study of social stratification primarily in the identification of speakers from different socioeconomic strata within city areas. Given this classification of the speaker, linguistic variables which have predictable variations in the speaker's performance in specified situations are identified. The eventual combined description of speaker, linguistic variable, situations, and range of variation (linguistic continuum) comprise the product of a typical urban language study.

The Attitude Variable

Most studies of relations between language and attitude represent a particular definition of the sociolinguistic situation. Specifically, there is the incorporation of a special interest upon the listener, because it is his attitudes that are often the focus of study, and there is a further concern with the particular definition of attitude as well as its measurement. Like language or speech, attitude is a concept susceptible to a variety of levels of analysis and measurement. In psychological terms, attitude is typically defined as some type of predisposition to behave or respond in a certain way. Some definitions of attitudes are so specific as to involve, say, a predicted approach to or avoidance of a stimulus. Others are so general that they could include all of the meanings a person might have for a concept. In the most general terms, the research literature on language and attitude involves such areas of investigation as the following:

1. Attitude studies concerning identifications of race and status usually note the appearance of certain stigmatized grammatical and phonological features that mark the speech of the lower socioeconomic groups, then try to relate these features to observations by listeners from various social strata and their ability to predict status and race from brief speech samples.

2. Studies of cultural stereotypes based on speech usually report the personality characteristics which people associate with different cultural or ethnic groups.

3. Occupational attitude studies usually focus on interpreting correlates between the social stratification of the linguistic variables and how listeners assign occupations to persons who speak in ways characteristic of different strata.

4. Finally, teachers' ratings of children's speech usually attempt to assess how teachers evaluate the speech of pupils, particularly in terms of their "sounding disadvantaged."

Although attitudinal studies of the foregoing types incorporate the linguistic variable, it is on the definition of this variable that similarity among studies ceases. Studies have represented language manipulations which vary all the way from the entire language which is being spoken to the manipulation of several individual pronunciation variations of a phoneme or phonemes. From the standpoint of research design, the language stimulus used in studies in this area typically represents what is called the *independent* variable in research designs. It is the causal variable, the one varied intentionally in experimental research designs. By contrast, the *dependent* variable is the variable said to be affected by variations in the independent variable. In language and attitude studies, variation in attitudes—as presumably caused by variations in the language variable—is the dependent variable.

Presumably, if a person is responding to the entire language which is being spoken (e.g., English as against French), attitudes will probably represent associations respondents have with this language as a whole as well as with the people who speak it. On the other hand, in studies where the language variations represent speakers of different social class, the problem is to determine which of the characteristics of the speech are affecting the attitudes of the respondent. To meet the demands of research design, there should be an attempt to ferret out from the language variable all characteristics except those which are hypothesized to be cues which affect attitudes. In some studies this has been done in exacting detail. Listeners have provided responses based upon hearing speech segments which are similar in all respects except for variation in the pronunciation of a given phoneme. On the other hand, the problem of presenting such refined variations is that the stimulus becomes more and more artificial. As a consequence, we cannot be sure that the attitudes gained in response to such stimuli are at all representative of real world situations. In general, then, the identification and manipulation of the language variables in studies of language and attitude represent a compromise. On the one hand there are the necessities of research design, on the other, language samples should be representative of some universe of speakers and discourse.

Although the literature on language and attitudes is difficult to classify in any one set of categories, it can be roughly arranged on a continuum which represents the degree of specification of a language variable. On the most general level, independent variables may represent entire languages or people who speak them, whereas on the most detailed level, language as the independent variable might represent variations in the feature of an individual phoneme. The literature discussed in Chapter 2 is organized along this continuum.

Sampling Attitudes

Whereas studies of the general type discussed thus far (and to be reviewed in Chapter 2) have involved an a priori definition of attitudes to be measured, most of the research in the present program (Chapters 3-6) has involved an attempt to identify and subsequently measure language attitudes existing in populations of listeners. Our general strategy in this can be summarized in the following steps:

1. *Adjective sampling.* Persons (in most cases teachers) whose attitudes are to be studied are administered stimulus material on a pilot study basis, then asked to engage in discussions and to comment freely about their reactions to the speakers. It is assumed that these reactions are reflective of the kinds of attitudes which persons hold toward what is represented in the stimulus (speech) materials. In particular, it is assumed that the adjectives used in their responses are representative of the types of attitudes held by the respondents. Thus, for

example, if teachers tended to talk about children sounding "fluent" or "disfluent," "standard," "clear," or "grammatical," it could be assumed that these are reflective of the attitudinal framework of their responses. From the context of these responses, adjectives are identified and considered for subsequent inclusion in attitude scales.

2. *The use of prototype attitude scales.* Adjectives obtained in Step 1 are then incorporated into a semantic differential scale format which defines a bipolar response continuum such as the following:

clear___ : ___ : ___ : ___ : ___ : ___ : ___ unclear

When a respondent is given a series of such scales to use in reaction to a stimulus, he is told that the positions nearest to the adjectives would indicate that he is treating the stimulus as either "highly" clear, or unclear. Checking one of the cells next to these extremes would indicate an association of the stimulus with a rating of "very" clear or unclear. Checking either cell adjacent to the center cell would indicate an association of "somewhat" clear or unclear. Finally, the center point on the scale is used to indicate an attitude .of "neither" clear, unclear, or a neutral point between the two adjectives. These types of scales follow from a more detailed psychological consideration of attitudes by Charles Osgood and his associates (Osgood, Suci, and Tannenbaum, 1957) who operationally define attitude as quantified sets of responses to bipolar scales.

Not all adjectives that are initially identified in Step 1 can be assigned opposites, and often there are cases of redundancy among potential scales. Accordingly, there is an editing process which takes place in selecting adjectives from the initial responses.[1]

3. *Identification of major dimensions of response.* Theoretically, a respondent's attitudes might be as detailed as all of the individual scales on the prototype instrument. Thus, if there are 25 different bipolar adjective scales, there conceivably could be 25 different attitudes. However, there are usually redundancies in the uses of the scales (sometimes very subtle) which reflect that a person is not rating the stimuli in an independent manner on each individual scale. In such cases, this is sometimes evidence that they are responding in terms of more basic, underlying dimensions of reaction, each of which may be reflected in several similar scales. For example, if it can be determined that persons fill in such scales as "fluency—disfluency, intelligible—unintelligible, standard—nonstandard," in a highly interrelated manner, this would probably

---

[1] Adjectival opposites can be obtained from the respondent population simply by presenting them with adjectives, either in oral or written form, and asking them to provide their own ideas of opposites. Where there is good consensus among respondents as to the opposites, this is a basis for defining a likely semantic differential scale.

TABLE 1.1

A Simplified Rotated Factor Matrix (Fictitious Data)

Scales	Factors	
	I	II
High (low) pitched	-.04	-.84
Intelligible (un-)	.88	.03
Strong (weak)	.38	.76
Fluent (dis-)	.76	-.06
Large (small)	.18	.69
Masculine (feminine)	.08	.78

mean that their attitudinal response is a single, more basic, underlying dimension that might be called "clarity."

It is possible mathematically to determine such interrelationships among scales by a technique known as *factor analysis.* Essentially, factor analysis allows the researcher to calculate indexes of interrelationships (correlations) among the uses of the scales, then to see whether there is evidence of some type of major clusters of usage of the scales. One of the major outcomes of a factor analysis is a *rotated factor matrix,* such as the simplified one shown in Table 1.1. Suppose, for example, that the same scales as mentioned above are involved in a study along with the further scales of "high pitched–low pitched, masculine–feminine, large–small, and strong–weak." Results of a factor analysis as shown in a rotated factor matrix would indicate: (1) whether underlying the usage of the various scales there are any factors (clustering of different scales), (2) how many factors (clusters) there are, and (3) the relationship of these factors with the individual scales.

In the example shown in Table 1.1 we have illustrated that two factors could be found in this analysis. The relationship of the individual scales with these two factors can be seen from the numerical indices found in the table, which are called *factor loadings.* Such a loading indicates the degree of relationship between individual scales and a factor. Here, "0.0" would mean no relationship, "+1.0" would mean a perfect positive relationship, and "-1.0" would mean a perfect inverse relationship. As can be seen in this example, scales relating to fluency and intelligibility are all positively related to factor 1, whereas those related to pitch and masculinity are related to factor 2. The results of this analysis would be grounds for assuming that in rating language samples for the different scales just mentioned, evaluations reflect only two basic dimensions of judgment instead of seven dimensions corresponding to the individual scales. The factors identified in the analysis give evidence that two judgmental dimensions are involved, and the relations of the individual scales with these two factors are a basis for interpreting the nature of these dimensions. In any analysis of the results, it would be more economical and accurate to summarize findings in terms of average scores on the two judgmental dimensions than it would be to average scores on the seven different individual scales. By the same token, in further research, one might proceed by using only two newly defined scales that would be reflective of these factors, or it would be possible to continue with all scales, but interpreting results (by using averages) in terms of how they reflect two underlying dimensions of judgment. Often, some type of compromise is made among these alternatives. That is, the researcher will proceed with a number of scales used to index each judgmental dimension so as to insure that persons' ratings represent different facets of each basic dimension, but at the same time, major redundancies among different scales may be reduced by omitting selected items.

All of the foregoing reflects a characteristic of the sociolinguistic study of linguistic attitudes that is unique to the programs of research reported in the Chicago (Chapter 3) and Texas (Chapter 4) studies. In a more abstract view, this reflects the strategy for identifying attitudes already existing in the behavior of listeners rather than imposing certain a priori definitions of attitude in the study.

Plan of the Monograph

Although research in our own program is not the direct extension of prior studies, it has been influenced by a number of characteristics of such studies. The goal of Chapter 2 is to describe some of this context, not so much as a comprehensive review of all research literature in this area but in the perspective most relevant to the present program of research.

As has been already mentioned, Chapters 3 and 4 are reports of research conducted in the midwest and in central Texas. The former involves development of semantic differential materials used with a group of Chicago inner city teachers in response to audiotapes. The major assessment was in terms of how these teachers rated children of different ethnicity and sex; a secondary focus was upon teacher differences in overall rating behaviors. In the Texas study the strategy was similar to that of Chicago, except that videotape stimulus materials were developed and both teacher and student populations included Mexican-Americans in addition to Blacks and Whites. Although the developmental procedures for a scaling instrument were again undertaken in the Texas research, the resulting instrument was very similar to that originally developed in the

Chicago research. There were several further additions in the Texas research. One was the assessment of the relationship between language attitudes and teachers' academic expectations of the children, and a separate attempt to measure teachers' stereotyped attitudes based upon having them fill out the rating scales in their response to their "experiences" with children of different ethnic groups. Finally, as in the Chicago research, analyses were also focused upon individual types of teachers in terms of rating behaviors.

Chapter 5 represents an additional area thought most important by the research team. Prior to this point all our research had involved attitude measures which reflected a person's marking a particular point on an attitude scale. The analysis then focused on mean attitudes. The new question was whether an attitude might be more of a spatial concept. That is, perhaps a person's attitude might also be accurately assessed as a *range* of ratings of a particular stimulus rather than a single midpoint. For example, a teacher might choose to rate a child's speech as somewhere between slightly nonstandard and markedly nonstandard. The "width" or "latitude" of that rating has particular significance when one considers stereotyped attitudes, closed-mindedness about racial stereotypes, and the like. Accordingly, an attempt was undertaken to measure such ranges, or what we call "latitude" of attitudes.

Chapter 6 represents additional research which has been conducted in relation to the mainstream projects. Some of these were methodological in nature; others were focused upon questions which arose in terms of attitude measures, stereotyping, and the application of some of these concepts to situations other than teachers per se. In all, Chapter 6 is a collection of individual research projects that might best be described as a potpourri.

chapter 2

PRIOR RESEARCH

Overview

The idea that listeners will make evaluations about a speaker's personality, ethnicity, education, intelligence, or even appearance merely from speech clues has received considerable support in the research literature of the social sciences. As mentioned in Chapter 1 the independent variables in this research have been stimuli characteristic of cues ranging all the way from speech in a given language to the details of particular dialects or styles. The dependent variables have been equally diverse, ranging from personality assessments to details about individual behaviors or traits. This chapter is essentially a review of research undertaken by persons other than those involved in our projects. As such it has provided an influential context and was of invaluable use in aiding our own research program. The discussion is arranged in terms of definitions of the linguistic variable.

Variations in the Language Spoken

Several studies have involved manipulation of which language is spoken (as an independent variable) and have sought relations with personality traits as a dependent variable. Perhaps the best known study of this type was conducted by Lambert and his colleagues (Lambert, Hodgson, Gardner, and Fillenbaum, 1960). In this study, French Canadian and English Canadian college students were presented tapes of bilingual speakers of French and English who had read aloud the same passage in two languages. They were asked to rate the speakers on fourteen traits such as leadership, sense of humor, self-confidence, height, and so on. Listeners, unaware that the same speaker was heard in the two languages, had only the language characteristics as cues for the personality judgments. Surprisingly, both French and English Canadians judged the speakers using the French guise less favorably than the same speaker using the English guise. These responses were interpreted by the researchers as evidence of a community-wide stereotype in which English Canadians were viewed more favorably. Thus it seems reasonable to conclude that the "matched guise"[1] speech samples elicit in the listener attitudes which he associates with the language group of which the speaker is a member.

A study by Preston (1963) demonstrated the effect of sex differences of both speaker and listener on personality judgments of the above type. In this instance English Canadian subjects evaluated French Canadian female speakers as generally more "confident," "intelligent," and "ambitious" than their English Canadian counterparts. However, the same judges showed a negative bias toward French Canadian males, although not as predominantly as in the 1960 study. On the other hand, French Canadian female listeners preferred the English Canadian female guises but found the French Canadian male guise more appealing than the English counterpart. Male French Canadians tended to rate both the male and female English speakers more positively than the French speakers.

Several studies have examined the evaluational reactions of children to determine the age at which stereotypes of different ethnic-language groups are acquired. Again using the matched guise technique, Anisfeld and Lambert (1964) presented monolingual and bilingual French Canadian 10-year-olds with taped speech samples. The children rated each speaker's personality on 15 traits. Results indicated that the monolingual (French-speaking) children upgraded the French voices, whereas the bilingual children showed less differentiation in their ratings of the French and English voices. The researchers suggest that at age ten the child has not been influenced by the cultural stereotype prevailing in the adult population and thus the ratings of the children were not similar to those obtained in the adult French population (as in Lambert, *et al.,* 1960).

Pursuing the question of when devaluation of their own linguistic community becomes apparent in French Canadian children, Lambert, Frankel, and Tucker (1966) asked French Canadian girls ranging in age from nine to eighteen to

---

[1]Problems of the matched guise technique are that only very skilled speakers can make an oral reading sound "natural," especially when varying language or dialect. Spontaneous speech contains many features—pausing, corrections, conversational interaction—which relate directly to linguistic attitudes. Oral reading, unless manipulated to sound so, omits these important details. On the other hand, oral reading in the matched guise technique does control for content in a much more rigorous fashion than can be done in spontaneous speech samples. The senior author's (F. W.) preference has been to try to control content cues by interviewing and editing techniques rather than trying to accommodate the problems of reading aloud.

evaluate the personality of French and English speakers presented in several passages. A comparison of the ratings of the matched guises revealed that a definite preference for the English guise began to emerge at age twelve, especially among bilinguals attending private schools.

An additional study (Lambert, Anisfeld, and Yeni-Komshian, 1965) involving differences between entire languages was conducted using the matched guise approach in the comparison of Hebrew and Arabic speech. Adolescents from Arab Israeli and Jewish Israeli groups rated both Hebrew and Arabic language samples. In rating their own and the other ethnic language samples, subjects did not follow the French and English Canadian patterns of stereotyping. That is, one linguistic community was not rated consistently less favorably by both groups. Rather, Hebrew listeners and Arabic listeners responded to representatives of the opposite group in a mutually unfavorable manner. For instance, both samples of subjects judged their own cultural group as more "reliable," "better looking," more "friendly," and the like.

In South America, Wölck (1972) used a semantic differential scale and an occupational suitability scale to determine attitudes toward Spanish and Quechua in bilingual Peru. The raters ranged in school level from late primary through the university, including a small group of teachers, and consisted of bilinguals dominant in Spanish, Quechua, or ambilinguals, and Spanish monolinguals. They were asked to rate both Quechua-Spanish bilinguals (in both guises) from the middle and lower classes and a middle-class Spanish monolingual. Among all raters, reactions were generally differentiated in the direction of associating Spanish with higher ratings on criteria of institutional reference such as "low-class—high-class," "educated—uneducated," and "urban—rural." Quechua was generally given higher ratings on criteria of affective value such as "ugly—pretty," "weak—strong," "kind—unkind." This seemed to indicate a strong native loyalty to Quechua, despite the stigma in reference to social status.

Variations in Dialect of the Speaker

A number of studies have involved variation in the dialect spoken, but most of these have involved variations in the speakers rather than the use of the matched guise technique. One of the first such studies (Putnam and O'Hern, 1955) involved both the description of dialect differences and a test of the importance of these differences in judging the social status of the speaker. The speech of members of a lower-class Negro urban area in Washington, D. C., was analyzed for the range of phonemic and syntactic deviations from "standard" English. Such linguistic phenomena as "weakened consonant articulation," the inclusion of "aberrant vowel and diphthong allophones" and "unsophisticated vocabulary and sentence structure" marked the major differences of this dialect group. Three speakers from this lower-class community and nine other speakers of varying higher social status were recorded after they had been read the fable of "The Lion and the Mouse" and were asked to retell it in their own words. These twelve speech samples were then arranged in random order and played to seventy untrained judges who were asked to rate the speakers' social status. Correlation between the judges' ratings and an objective index (Warner's Index of Social Status) was .80. The fact that respondents produced such accurate judgments of the speakers' status on the basis of short speech samples emphasizes the importance of dialect cues in social class identifications.

Harms (1963) using the same speech samples obtained by Putnam and O'Hern in a Negro area of Washington, D. C., elicited responses from midwestern college students regarding the social status of the twelve speakers. Although the midwestern group, unlike the untrained judges in the East, were unaware that the speakers were Negro, the status differentiations were much the same. That is, status dialects were recognized regardless of the race of the speaker. Similarly, although the judges were from two different regions of the country their identification of social status of the speaker was highly correlated with an objective index of status. It becomes clear that dialect differences and the social prestige which they may possess are sometimes not restricted to any particular region of the country.

In another study, Harms (1961) varied not only the status of the speakers but also the status of the listeners. Subjects in the Columbus, Ohio, area were classed into three groups using the Hollingshead Two-Factor Index of Status Position. One-minute speech samples from three speakers in each of the three status groups (high, middle, low) served as stimuli. Non-college adult listeners from each of the three status groups rated the speakers' status and credibility. Results indicated that listeners of all statuses rated speakers in accordance with the objective index and that listeners, regardless of status, judged high social status speakers to be more credible than low status speakers. The consistency of judgments across status boundaries provides additional evidence of the significance of dialect differences. Moe (1972) replicated and extended this study to conclude that objectively measured speaker's status and subjectively perceived speaker's status may be significantly correlated just on the basis of minimal phonological variables.

Tucker and Lambert (1969) assessed relations between different American dialect groups and attitudes. Taped speech samples representative of six American-English dialect groups (Network, Educated White, Educated southern Negro, Mississippi Peer, Howard University, New York Alumni) were played to three groups of college students (northern White, southern White, southern Negro). The students were asked to evaluate the speech samples using an adjective check list describing personality characteristics the speaker might possess and also to rank the dialects in order of their preference. Evaluators of both regions and races rated a dialect typical of "network newscasters" most favorably. Educated southern Negro was rated next most favorably by northern White and southern Black listeners. The southern White students, in contrast, rated educated southern White as the second most favorable. Northern and southern White evaluators agreed in their ratings of the Mississippi Peer dialect as the least desirable; the Negro students, however, described the educated southern White as the least favorable. These findings tended to support the social stereotyping thesis suggested in earlier research (Lambert, et al., 1960) in which ratings of speech samples elicit attitudes that different ethnic groups hold toward one another. As an extension of the Tucker-Lambert experiment, Fraser (1972) duplicated that study and discovered in addition that the listener's judgment of speaker's race is correlated with his overall evaluation of the speaker.

A study by Buck (1968) involved racial identification of speakers, in addition to general attitudinal ratings of "competence" and "trustworthiness." College students were asked to listen to tapes of White and Negro New York speech judged to be variations of "standard" and "nonstandard" English. On several attitude measures the students expressed a preference for the speakers of "standard" dialect. Additionally, the Negro speaker of standard dialect was judged by 24 out of 26 subjects as being White. However, there was no confusion in distinguishing the Negro "nonstandard" speech from the White "nonstandard" speech. Ratings of trustworthiness and competence were also elicited from the listeners as a measure of the speakers' overall credibility. Competence ratings favored standard speakers and showed no race differences. Trustworthiness ratings showed a mixed pattern. Standard dialect speakers of both races were judged more favorably, but the Negro nonstandard speaker was rated more trustworthy than his White counterpart.

A further study (Anisfeld, Bogo, and Lambert, 1962) of this type involved the matched guise technique where the variation was between Jewish accented and nonaccented speech samples. Bidialectical speakers were recorded once in standard (Canadian) English and again in Jewish accented English. Results indicated that gentile listeners responded less favorably to a speaker when he was using Jewish accented speech. However, Jewish listeners evidenced variation in their evaluations of persons with Jewish accents. On certain personality traits they were judged more favorably, while on other characteristics they were devaluated.

Research similar to that of Lambert has also been carried out in Britain by Strongman and Woosley (1967), Cheyne (1970), and Giles (1971). In each study listeners who spoke various British dialects were asked to evaluate tapes of speakers of their own dialect and others. Results tend to support Lambert's findings that speakers of a standard dialect (in this case "perceived pronunciation") are evaluated by all listeners as more competent and intelligent than the nonstandard or regional speakers; however, the latter are perceived by all as friendlier, more honest and socially attractive than the former.

Bourhis, Giles, and Lambert (1972) used the matched guise technique in Quebec and Wales to ascertain listener's reactions to shifts in speech style to accommodate various social situations. In both cultures speakers who shifted speech styles toward the standard when speaking with a standard speaker were perceived as more intelligent.

Children's assessments of personality characteristics as well as race and occupation were examined by Bouchard-Ryan (1969). Fifth and sixth graders listened to tapes from the Detroit Dialect Study (Shuy, Wolfram, and Riley, 1967; cf. below in this chapter) and ranked the dialects in descending order: middle-class White, lower-class White, and lower-class Negro, respectively, while occupational levels were consistent with these differences. They were, however, only able to identify race correctly for the middle-class Whites and the lower-class Blacks.

Just as Lambert, Hodgson, Gardner, and Fillenbaum (1960, cf. this chapter) found French Canadians to rank English guises higher than the French guises of the same speaker; students, teachers and workers in French-speaking Canada also devalued their French in relationship to European French in a similar study by d'Anglejan and Tucker (1972). Furthermore, all groups indicated awareness of French-Canadian social class variations in dialect.

Studies of Teacher Attitudes

There have been various studies where the language stimulus materials came from pupils and the attitudes studied were those of teachers. Most such studies have appeared during the progress of our own program of research in the area. None represents any close coordination between our projects and theirs; most became known to us after they were completed and reports disseminated. It may be expected that these studies, like ours, traded somewhat upon the implications of Rosenthal and Jacobson's (1968) *Pygmalion in the Classroom*. That is, there has been an interest in teachers' linguistic attitudes because presumably such attitudes may affect the teacher's expectations of the children and, as a consequence, affect the children's progress in school. We will briefly mention several of these studies as part of the context of our own research. We will not, however, introduce our studies at this point since they are the topics of Chapters 3 and 4.

A number of teacher studies have involved use of the semantic differential technique in rating tapes of various dialect features. That these attitudes are dependent on the race of the teacher as well as on the social dialect and race of the child was well documented by Guskin (1970). One of the important results was that although Black and White teachers were in general agreement regarding judgments of speakers, Black teachers had a more positive orientation than White teachers toward middle-class speakers. Both groups evaluated Black speakers and working- and lower-class speakers less highly than White and middle-class speakers. Perkins (1970) also found that teachers held negative attitudes toward Black dialect speakers.

Hewett (1970), extending Tucker and Lambert's experiment (1969) with college students, found prospective White teachers also ready to devalue the speech of Black lower-class speakers, suggesting that such stereotyping exists before the teacher actually comes into much contact with the children.

The manner in which teachers form attitudes concerning children was the central focus in a recent study by Seligman, Tucker, and Lambert (1972). A variety of independent variables—photographs, speech samples, drawings, and compositions from third-grade boys—were examined for their role in attitude formation. Samples of these items were obtained from 36 children from working-class and upper-class families in the Montreal area. Each of these samples was then evaluated by student-teachers using seven-point scales appropriate to the matter being evaluated. For example, when evaluating the children's compositions the scales included an item such as: "The plot is: simple—complex." When evaluating the voices, items such as "Speed of speech is: quick—slow," "Pronunciation is: inarticulate—articulate," were included. On the basis of the student-teachers' ratings, eight drawings and eight compositions were chosen, four from those considered to be poor in quality and four considered good in quality. The selection of eight speech samples was based on the degree to which they were rated as sounding or looking "intelligent" or "unintelligent." Then all combinations of "poor" characteristics were made, with the exception that a good drawing was always paired with a good composition, and together these were taken as one unit of evaluation.

In the main experiment, each combination of characteristics was taken to represent a different hypothetical child. Eight children in all were "devised." Nineteen education majors, serving as subjects, were then presented with the eight children's photographs, speech samples, drawings, and compositions for their examination and evaluation. Subjects were asked to form an overall impression of each child and to rate him on a set of semantic differential scales similar to those used previously (e.g., "The child seems: intelligent—unintelligent"). Analysis of the scores on each rating scale revealed that those children who were rated as sounding intelligent also were rated significantly more favorably on other dimensions such as being "friendlier," "happier," "more enthusiastic," and so on. Similarly, those students judged from photographs as looking more intelligent were also thought to be significantly more "privileged," "happier," "more self-confident," and better students than those who were rated as looking unintelligent. Also, the effect of a good composition and drawing was shown in those students being rated significantly more intelligent, better students, and more enthusiastic than those boys with poor drawings and compositions.

Frender and Lambert (1972) suggest that a child's speech style may influence a teacher's assignment of grades for him.[2]

Variations in Individual Linguistic Cues

Recent urban language research in the United States has sometimes involved the study of associations between language characteristics that have been found to be socially stratified and the kinds of attitudes that respondents will relate to such characteristics. Such studies tend to examine two sides of the same coin regarding the phenomena of linguistic stratification. If the social or stylistic variations of a linguistic feature are correlated with the social stratification of its users, then it seems reasonable that such features may be cues when listeners judge the social status of a speaker.

Labov (1966), in a study of New York City speech, sought to determine which variations of pronunciation in a linguistic community were socially significant. In field studies, five phonological variables (/r/, /æ/, /ɔ/, /θ/, /ð/) were systematically examined to determine their appearance when stylistic and contextual situations were held constant.

On the basis of preliminary data, Labov (1966, p. 64) predicted that: "if any two subgroups of New York City speakers are ranked in a scale of social stratification, then they will be ranked in the same order by their differential use of /r/." To test this hypothesis, samples of the pronunciation of /r/ were elicited from sales personnel in three large Manhattan department stores representative of the top, middle, and bottom of the fashion and price scales. The assumption underlying this choice was that the employees of a store attempt to share in the status of the clientele and therefore persons working in the highest ranked store will emulate the speech of its customers rather than the speech of New York sales personnel in general. In a subtle manner, the interviewer asked 264 clerks for the location of an item which he knew to be located on the fourth floor, thus eliciting the utterance "fourth floor" in a natural conversational style. He followed their reply with the question, "Excuse me?" to elicit the same reply in a stressed utterance. The four occurrences of /r/ in the utterances "fourth floor"

[2]This information is based on an account by Bourhis, Giles, and Lambert (1972) of Frender, R. and Lambert, E. E. "The influence of pupils' speech styles on teacher evaluations." 23rd Annual Round Table Meeting, Georgetown, Washington, D. C., 1972.

served as the dependent variable, which was then rated on the basis of a previously devised binary scale. An (r-1) was entered for each case of a plainly constricted pronunciation; (r-0) for each case of unconstricted schwa, lengthening vowel, or no representation. In general, the results revealed a stratification of the pronunciation of /r/ similar to the stratification of the department stores. That is, the employees of the highest ranked store also were ranked highest in their use of (r-1) in both casual and emphatic situations. This evidence tends to confirm the thesis that certain detailed variations in phonemes (in this particular instance /r/) are indicators of status.

In a second field study, Labov (1966) dealt with stylistic variation. Again, the five phonological variables were elicited from speakers in several contexts (e.g., "casual speech," "word lists") and their stylistic variation was analyzed. This analysis revealed that certain phonological features varied consistently across social class lines. Labov postulated that these same variables might serve as cues for listeners in determining a speaker's social status. The task then became one of presenting listeners with samples of speech containing different variations of each phonological variant in a certain social strata and the rating of a speaker on an occupational scale. Listeners, after hearing sentences containing variants, rated the speaker according to his probable occupation ranging from "television personality" to "factory worker." This test of the subjective evaluation of phonological variables supported the correlation between the appearance of a phonological variant in a certain social strata and the rating of a speaker exhibiting that variant in a similar social strata. Labov concluded that when listeners are given speech samples containing these socially significant variables, they are able to determine the social class of the speaker.

Shuy, Baratz, and Wolfram's (1969) research added an additional variable to this line of investigation. They were primarily concerned with the effect that race and socioeconomic status of the listener has on the identification of the race and socioeconomic status of the speaker. Speech samples, 20 to 30 seconds in length, which exhibited dialect and pronunciation cues typical of male Negro and White speakers in the Detroit area served as stimuli in this study. The speakers represented four social classes: upper-middle, lower-middle, upper-working, and lower-working. Listeners were drawn from a wide spectrum of Detroit residents, including Negro and White sixth graders, eleventh graders, and adults of both sexes from four social strata. The response instrument included judgments of the speaker's race and a rating of the speaker's educational/ occupational level in addition to several semantic differential items.

Regarding the effect of socioeconomic status, results indicated that middle-class listeners were more accurate as judges of social class than were lower-class respondents. However, considering the speaker's socioeconomic status, it appears that the lower the status of the speaker the more accurately he is identified by listeners regardless of their socioeconomic status. In other words, subjects had little difficulty in recognizing the speech of a lower status speaker.

The variable of race tends to follow a somewhat similar pattern, that is, the lower the socioeconomic status of Black speakers the more accurate were the listeners' identification of race. In general, Blacks were identified correctly 80% of the time and Whites 81% of the time on the basis of only 30 seconds of speech. From the above data, the researchers concluded that the most outstanding fact in the differentiation of social dialects in Detroit is the presence of stigmatized grammatical and phonological features which are usually present in the speech of lower-class and ethnic groups. The speech of the middle class is typified by the absence of these features. In other words, lower-class speakers provide more salient cues from which the listener (regardless of his race or socioeconomic status) can differentiate, and these cues are tied to the education/occupation level of the speaker.

The importance of determining linguistic correlates of attitudes can be seen in the recent studies which have tried to ascertain what speech cues, if any, might be most relevant to the employer in hiring.

Shuy (1970) asked employers in Washington, D. C. to rank taped speech samples of Washington, D. C. Negro males by job categories. These samples were from all social classes, both adults and teenagers. Although the employers said that a man's speech had little to do with employment decisions, they consistently ranked the Black men who were actually doctors, professors, and architects in the same lower categories (fourth and fifth categories on a seven-place scale) with salesmen, policemen, and mechanics.

Determining which linguistic cues might be relevant to a hiring decision was the subject of a study by Findley (1972). Some 25 employers from major corporations in the Minneapolis-St. Paul area rated brief speech samples of White speakers from their region. Independent variables were the presence, absence, type, and frequency of occurrence of nonstandard grammatical features as well as the level of structural complexity. Employability was predicted by the first three variables.

However, it is not very clear whether determining which speech cues in Black speech a White employer is reacting to is a relevant question. In a study by Baird (1969) an attempt was made to isolate which linguistic features of Black speech in Austin, Texas, were relevant to employment decisions in the area. However in a pre-test, White raters who were not employers were unable to perceive any differences when the cues were manipulated, apparently indicating that a stereotype (Oh, she's a Negro) was immediately evoked by other linguistic cues of ethnicity, and raters failed to listen to the rest of the segments, which contained manipulated social dialect features. It remains to be seen what distinctions Black raters would have perceived. Perhaps Baird's findings can in part account for Shuy's observations that upper-class Black speech was downgraded by White employers.

It should be noted in passing, that one project in our series involved the development of semantic differential scales for use by employment interviewers who responded to audiotape speech samples. This study is reported in Chapter 6.

Some Final Notes

Probably the most rewarding generalization of the studies reviewed in this chapter is that very definite relations can be found between particular variations of language and the attitudes of listeners. In other words, most studies have been able to draw conclusions that have some degree of applicability to types of speech and the reactions of listeners. This line of research also provides a number of ideas for strategies in this area of study and at the same time is a basis for anticipating a variety of potential research shortcomings.

One problem is when the language variable is insufficiently identified. For example, if variations in accent are studied, not only the accent should be identified, but the linguistic variations present on the stimulus material should be described. It is also important for the listener to have some conception of whom the speech in a sample was intended for, as well as the conditions under which the sample was obtained. If teachers are to evaluate children's speech, it would obviously make a great deal of difference whether they thought that such speech was obtained under classroom as against playground conditions. When stimulus materials are eventually prepared, there will have to be a compromise between having well-defined variations in these materials yet not increasing their artificiality to an extent that any attitudes related to them have no generality to the real world. This is a compromise between the satisfactory requirements of experimental design, where one variable can be manipulated at a time, as against making some generalizations about language which, in effect, is a naturally complex pattern of variables changing across time.

Finally, there is a problem of the conceptual as well as operational definition of attitude. The literature of psychology is not an especially good basis for delimiting the *concept* of attitude, and researchers are, for the most part, confined to their operational definitions. Beyond the measurement problem is the need to make assumptions about the operation of the attitudinal process. When a person responds to a speech sample, does he carefully perceive the details of that sample and then mark the rating scales in accordance with what he perceives? Or might this process be one of a person responding to several cues in a stimulus which elicit a stereotype about people who speak that way, so that the attitude ratings may directly reflect this stereotype? In short, the question is the degree to which ratings represent a careful assessment of the stimulus materials as against a reporting of personal stereotypes. As can be seen in Chapter 3, the report of the Chicago study, this issue is raised on a *post hoc* basis in the interpretation of the findings. It became a more direct focus for investigation in the Texas studies (Chapter 4), eventually to the point of attempting to measure stereotyped attitudes.

chapter 3

THE CHICAGO RESEARCH

The Chicago research represented our first major effort in the series of studies to be reported in detail in this monograph. The idea for the study was formulated at the time the senior researcher was involved in a series of studies focused upon quantitative analyses of language performance in selected tapes that had been drawn from the corpus of the Detroit dialect study. Given the description of a variety of characteristics of these tapes, and how these characteristics differentiated children according to social status and ethnicity, the question was raised whether these tapes might also be differentiated upon the basis of listener attitudes—particularly teacher-listener attitudes. Plans were undertaken for gathering attitude data on each of these tapes and investigating the degree to which children's differences of social status and ethnicity could be predicted upon the basis of attitudinal measures. This reasoning was prompted somewhat by Labov's (1966) earlier research where he reasoned that if selected speech samples in New York City could be socially stratified upon the basis of given linguistic characteristics, these same characteristics presented to listeners should be a basis for the listeners differentiating among the social statuses of the speakers. Initial planning of our study was also influenced by earlier work by Putnam and O'Hern (1955) and by Harms (1961) who both found relatively high correlations between the status differentiation of stimulus tapes and ratings of social status provided by listeners. There was also the major and influential work of Wallace Lambert and his colleagues (1960) who by using the matched guise techniques had revealed stereotype attitudes of French and English Canadians toward each other, based upon the ratings of speech samples. Given a background of such studies, and the availability of tapes for which characteristics had already been identified, the design of this first teacher attitude study was focused mainly upon methods for the development of attitude measures, gathering such measures, then comparing such measures with the types of children and characteristics of their speech samples.

In this chapter, we present an edited report of the Chicago research originally published in the *Journal of Speech and Hearing Research* (Williams, 1970). A year or so after this research was conducted, we were increasingly pondering the question of the degree of generality of findings about linguistic attitudes to individual teachers. Results had indicated that overall averages could be calculated and generalizations made about attitudes of teachers as a group. But there was still the question of the degree of homogeneity among teachers. Further analysis of the data using Q-method was undertaken by Naremore (1971). The onput of this further analysis is the topic of the second half of this chapter.

On Sounding Disadvantaged[1]

The first steps in the Chicago research involved the development of the semantic differential scales according to the procedure which was generally outlined in Chapter 1 of this monograph. The following section reports in detail how this procedure was carried out.

Research Design

Speaker and listener populations. Although the details of the Detroit study are presented elsewhere (cf. Chapter 2 and Shuy, *et al.*, 1967), a few of its features are particularly pertinent to the present research, as they were the basis for the language sample in the Chicago study and other related research discussed in this monograph. The Detroit study was based upon a multiple-step, random sampling procedure. Some 200 fourth, fifth, and sixth-grade children were selected as part of the main sample of the original study.[2] Each child's family was assigned a value on the socioeconomic index incorporating a weighted combination of education, occupation, and residence factors.[3] Each interview was conducted in the child's home by a trained linguistic field worker who followed a predetermined schedule. Within this schedule was a section,

---

[1] Results of this study are also reported in Williams (1970).

[2] Counting interviews with family members, this main sample (called the *base* sample) included 545 persons. A further series of interviews (called the ethnic sample) was not considered in the present research.

[3] August B. Hollingshead and Fredrick C. Redlich, *Social Class and Mental Illness* (New York, 1958).

designed to take about 40 minutes, which was devoted to getting the child to talk freely on the topics of games and leisure, school, job aspirations, group structure, and fighting-accidents-illness. The field work was done by Shuy and his field staff during the summer of 1966.

In the Chicago study, speech samples from 40 fifth- and sixth-grade children were selected from sound tapes of the original Detroit study. These were obtained by randomly selecting pairs of Negro and White children (matched by sex and socioeconomic index) from the relatively low and middle-to-high ranges of the socioeconomic distribution of informants from the parent study. This procedure resulted in subsamples of 20 children each, classified as our H. S. (higher status) and L. S. (lower status) groups respectively. Within each of these groups were balanced subsamples (N = 10) of Negro and White children, and within each of these, balanced subsamples (N = 5) of males and females.[4] The selections used from these tapes had come from a portion of the linguistic interviews (see Shuy, et al., 1967, Part II) in which the field worker prompted the child to talk freely about selected topics. For this study, field worker-child interactions on two topics were selected:

Games (What kinds of games do you play around here?") As noted in the interview questionnaire, the field worker was supposed to note each game, to ask how it was played, and to get descriptions for such items as the "goal," "how to decide who is it," what to do "when a new person comes," etc.

TV ("What are your favorite TV programs?") Here the field worker tried to elicit the description of a recent episode.

The speech on each topic averaged 250 words per child but varied considerably among individual children. These 40 tapes had been employed in two earlier studies of this project. One involved the assessment of syntactic elaboration in the samples (Williams and Naremore, 1969b); the other centered on the analysis of the functional aspects of the children's speech (Williams and Naremore, 1969a).[5] As a consequence of these earlier studies, a variety of speech and language measures (described later) was readily available for use here.

---

[4]More of the characteristics of these children, their families, residential area, and the like, may be obtained by referring to their individual interview-tape numbers in the Detroit study (Shuy, et al., "Linguistic Correlates of Social Stratification in Detroit Speech"). These tape numbers were: 0459, 0647, 0306, 0287, 0092, 0345, 0686, 0291, 0172, 0097, 0070, 0547, 0228, 0364, 0666, 0152, 0008, 0288, 0060, 0149, 0609, 0299, 0682, 0423, 0563, 0379, 0475, 0557, 0491, 0263, 0614, 0486, 0153, 0220, 0604, 0120, 0517, 0688, 0290, 0495.

[5]These earlier studies involved an additional topic, "Aspirations" ("What do you want to be when you finish school?") which, because of limits in our testing design and the expense of additional language coding, was not used in the present project.

The listener sample (the teachers) was obtained largely by convenience. It consisted of 33 primary school teachers, all from schools in inner-city Chicago, who were attending a summer institute in speech and language. Despite this selection by convenience, it was felt that this sample represented a type of listener who played a significant role in the lives of the types of children represented in the speaker tapes. There was no reason to expect vast differences between the types of children's speech in Detroit and Chicago. (The fact that in informal discussion after hearing the tapes, the teachers would try to guess the Chicago school attended by a child was evidence that the difference in cities was of little consequence for our study.) A promise to the teachers of anonymity prevents a description of them in detail. Of the total, three were males, and no attempt was made to conduct separate analyses of this division. However, for purposes of comparative analysis, the response data were divided according to the race of the teacher. The researcher made this classification on the basis of his own observations since the institute carried no records on this; 12 teachers were identified as Negro (T_n), 21 as White (T_w).

Semantic differential. Generally as described in Chapter 1, a procedure was undertaken where samples of the stimulus tapes were administered to the small groups of subjects who were encouraged to speak freely about the children whom they heard. From these conversations a variety of adjectives and their referents were identified, and a set of prototype scales was developed. This set of scales is presented in Table 3.1. These 22 scales were the ones used in the main study of the Chicago teachers.

Testing procedure. Response data from at least six teachers were obtained for each of the 80 stimulus tapes. This was accomplished by dividing (by lot) the teachers into five subgroups of listeners, and by assigning 16 tapes to each subgroup. Each set of 16 tapes represented 16 subsets of the language sample (all combinations of the two levels of status, sex, race, and topic). This assignment of subsets to listener groups was based on a Latin-square type of design. Testing took place in four one-half hour sessions in which four tapes were played and rated in each session. These sessions were incorporated into the institute's schedule during the first four days of classes.

Each listener was provided with a 16-page booklet of semantic differential scales, sufficient for responding to his quota of the tapes. These 16 pages represented the random combination of three permutations (scale order and scale polarity) of the format shown in Table 3.1, done to avoid order effects. This booklet was distributed just prior to each listening session (i.e., the four tapes for a day) and collected at its conclusion.

Testing took place simultaneously in five different listening suites, each equipped for tape playback and supervised by one of the assistants working for the institute. Prior to the first day's testing, oral directions on use of the

TABLE 3.1
The Semantic Differential Format

WORD USAGES ARE:
*consistently
   incorrect __ : __ : __ :__ :__ : __ : __ consistently correct

THE CHILD IS:
highly fluent __ : __ : __ : __ :__ :__ : __ highly disfluent*

THE CHILD SOUNDS:
*male-like __ : __ : __ : __ :__ :__ : __ female-like

THE MEANING OF THE MESSAGE IS:
*very unclear __ : __ :__ :__ : __ : __ : __ very clear

PRONUNCIATION IS:
*nonstandard __ : __ : __ : __ :__ : __ : __ standard

SENTENCES ARE:
complex-
   elaborated __ : __ : __ : __ : __ : __ : __ simple-unelaborated*

THE CHILD USES LANGUAGE:
effectively __ : __ :__ :__ : __ : __ : __ ineffectively*

THE CHILD'S FAMILY IS PROBABLY:
*low social
   status __ : __ : __ : __ : __ :__ : __ high social status

THE AGE OF THE CHILD IS: seven, eight, nine, ten, eleven, twelve,
thirteen, fourteen

THE CHILD'S SPEECH INDICATES:
*a poor educational
   background __ : __ : __ : __ : __ :__ : __ a good one

VOCABULARY IS:
sophisticated __ : __ :__ :__ : __ : __ : __ unsophisticated*

THE MESSAGE PERSPECTIVE IS:
seldom tied to
   speaker __ : __ :__ :__ : __ : __ : __ solely tied to him*

*These asterisks define the pole of the scale assigned a value of "1" in the quantification
scheme. The asterisks did not appear on the actual instrument.

TABLE 3.1 (continued)

THE OVERALL MESSAGE IS:
*disorganized __ : __ : __ : __ : __ : __ : __ organized

SENTENCES ARE:
*fragmentary __ : __ : __ : __ : __ : __ : __ complete

THE CHILD SOUNDS CULTURALLY:
*disadvantaged __ : __ : __ : __ : __ : __ : __ advantaged

THE MESSAGE IS:
rich in detail __ : __ : __ : __ : __ : __ : __ sparse in detail*

THE CHILD SOUNDS:
*White-like __ : __ : __ : __ : __ : __ : __ Negro-like

THE CHILD SEEMS:
*reticent to speak __ : __ : __ : __ : __ : __ : __ eager to speak

THE CHILD SOUNDS:
confident __ : __ : __ : __ : __ : __ : __ unsure*

THE LANGUAGE SHOWS A:
standard American
    style __ : __ : __ : __ : __ : __ : __ marked ethnic style*

PRONUNCIATION IS:
*unclear-indistinct __ : __ : __ : __ : __ : __ : __ clear-distinct

THE GRAMMAR IS:
*quite bad __ : __ : __ : __ : __ : __ : __ quite good

---

*These asterisks define the pole of the scale assigned a value of "1" in the quantification scheme. The asterisks did not appear on the actual instrument.

---

semantic differential and explanation of the testing sessions were given to the teachers as a group. Nothing was said about any of the actual characteristics of the children on the tapes. The teachers were told that the listening sessions were a part of the institute's program, and they were assured of anonymity for their individual ratings.

   Data tabulation. Response data on the semantic differentials were quantified by the arbitrary (but consistent) assignment of the digits one through seven to correspond with the pole marked by an asterisk in Table 3.1. Subsequently collated with these response data on a child-by-topic basis were the characteristics of the language samples as tabulated from prior studies (Williams and

Naremore, 1969a, b), and selected characteristics additionally identified for this project.

Dimensionality of judgments. As discussed earlier, a first question was whether a pattern of scale interrelations would be found in the response data, and if so, whether it would be interpretable as a judgmental model. For this, separate intercorrelation matrices were initially calculated for the T_n and T_w response data. The 22 scales served as variables in the analyses, and children-by-topic-by-teacher served as replicates ($N_{T_n} = 192$, $N_{T_w} = 336$). Both matrices were subsequently factored by the principal components procedure and the raw matrix subjected to varimax rotation. For purposes of comparative interpretation, the results of the T_n and T_w analyses are combined in Table 3.2.

TABLE 3.2

Rotated Factor Matrices for Analyses of Negro (T_n)
and White (T_w) Teacher Responses to
the Semantic Differential Scales

Variables	Factors							
	I		II		III		IV	
	T_n	T_w	T_n	T_w	T_n	T_w	T_n	T_w
1. word use (incorr.)*	0.30	0.51	0.73	0.44	-0.11	0.30	0.01	0.09
2. child is (disfl.)	0.50	0.75	0.53	0.31	0.05	0.27	-0.70	-0.03
3. child sounds (male)	0.11	0.05	0.06	0.16	-0.26	0.29	0.77	-0.76
4. meaning (unclear)	0.62	0.75	0.16	0.26	-0.14	-0.07	0.27	-0.06
5. pronoun. (nonstd.)	0.45	0.45	0.70	0.70	0.06	-0.02	0.13	-0.09
6. sentences (simp.)	0.63	0.49	0.39	0.33	0.21	0.55	0.00	0.07
7. lang. (ineffect.)	0.64	0.75	0.59	0.42	0.04	0.16	0.00	-0.05
8. family (low status)	0.52	0.51	0.67	0.69	0.27	0.21	0.18	0.07

*The words in parentheses indicate the pole assigned the value of 1.0 for the scale.

TABLE 3.2 (continued)

9. age (seven)	0.08	0.00	-0.02	0.05	-0.25	0.34	-0.66	0.77
10. speech (good) backg.)	0.54	0.56	0.64	0.65	0.08	0.15	0.25	0.05
11. vocab. (unsoph.)	0.58	0.44	0.60	0.45	0.05	0.40	-0.01	0.10
12. perspect. (speaker)	-0.02	0.07	0.05	0.02	0.85	0.70	0.00	-0.01
13. message (disorg.)	0.60	0.80	0.46	0.25	-0.06	0.01	-0.02	-0.05
14. sentences (frag.)	0.58	0.76	0.41	0.20	0.40	0.26	0.06	0.00
15. culturally (disad.)	0.46	0.56	0.64	0.68	0.20	0.22	0.23	0.02
16. message det. (sparse)	0.82	0.66	0.19	0.32	0.19	0.41	-0.07	-0.01
17. child is (White)	0.20	-0.01	-0.69	-0.86	0.06	-0.10	0.12	0.11
18. child is (reticent)	0.77	0.73	0.05	0.11	-0.10	0.36	-0.02	-0.13
19. child is (unsure)	0.80	0.82	0.28	0.12	-0.02	0.14	-0.05	0.08
20. language (ethnic)	0.26	0.22	0.69	0.86	0.34	0.12	-0.06	-0.08
21. pronoun. (unclear)	0.58	0.59	0.60	0.52	-0.05	-0.08	0.16	-0.08
22. grammar (bad)	0.47	0.59	0.73	0.55	-0.01	0.00	0.12	0.01
(Percentage total variance)	(27%)	(32%)	(26%)	(23%)	(06%)	(08%)	(06%)	(06%)

*The words in parentheses indicate the pole assigned the value of 1.0 for the scale.

As can be seen in Table 3.2, the factors defined in the T_n and T_w results are substantially similar. Both analyses yielded four factors, two of which were relatively major (both accounting for slightly over 50% of the total variance in each analysis), and two of which were minor (< 8% each). Scale loadings on factors III and IV prompted the same interpretations for both sets of response data. Factor III was clearly and solely a reflection of the independence of the message perspective (scale-12) ratings. Factor IV was a reflection of an inverse relation between ratings of age (scale-9) and sex (scale-3). Although it might seem tempting to have interpreted these minor factors further, both were relatively negligible in terms of percentage of total variance, and factor IV overly accentuated the relatively low correlations between age and sex in the data ($r = 0.11$ in the T_n data, -0.21 in T_w). Since neither factor reflected any relation to judgments of the child's social status, they were omitted from further consideration.

Because of their relatively high proportion of extracted variance and because of their relation to the social status scales (8, 10, and 15), factors I and II were the main foci for interpretation in this phase of the analyses. Here the question was whether they contained sufficient evidence to pose a two-factor judgmental model. In both T_n and T_w analyses, factor I appeared symptomatic of gross ratings of what might tentatively be called "confidence-eagerness" owing mainly to the relatively high loadings of the scales unsure—confident (19) and reticent—eager (18). Although there were further scales correlating substantially with this factor in the two data sets, most could be interpreted as meaningfully related to this gross dimension. Differences between the two data sets on such scales were considered reflective of speech characteristics to which the two groups of teachers may have been sensitive in making a confidence-eagerness judgment—for example, message detail (16) for Negro teachers, or fluency (2) for White teachers. Factor II in both data sets was a reflection of a kind of "ethnicity-nonstandardness" rating, although ethnicity may have been more of a central correlate of this dimension in the White teachers' ratings, as compared with those of the Negro teachers. In both data sets, standardness of pronunciation (5) was a relatively high loading scale. However, the relatively high loadings of word use (1) and grammar (22) ratings in the T_n results were not found in the T_w results.

Disregarding the minor factors (III and IV), the foregoing analyses and interpretations pointed to a two-dimension judgmental model, presumably underlying the teachers' use of the semantic differential scales. In more practical terms the implication was that teachers had grossly differentiated the children along two main and relatively independent dimensions tentatively labeled as confidence-eagerness (factor I) and ethnicity-nonstandardness (factor II). Some differences, however, between the scale loadings on the two factors in the T_w and T_n data sets foreshadowed teacher differences in judgmental behavior.

Social status judgments. As can be seen in Table 3.2, the three scales (8, 10, 15) which were thought to encompass the teachers' ratings of social status were correlated with both factors I and II, indicating that such ratings were associated with both dimensions of the judgmental model. The similar intercorrelation patterns of these three scales with factors in both data sets, coupled with the observation that the zero-order correlations among the scales were all between 0.78 and 0.85, prompted the conclusion that the teachers had differentiated little among these particular scales—that is, they had given a similar gross rating of social status on each. Accordingly, for subsequent analyses the data on the three status scales were combined (summed) as a single variable labeled status-judgment.

At this point, the reasoning was that teachers' status-judgment ratings could be incorporated into a two-factor model such as was initially defined by factors I and II in Table 3.2 and by the loadings of the social status ratings of these factors. A more general description, however, was provided by the calculation of a multiple determination coefficient (R^2) and its variance components, based upon a three-variable linear equation of the regression of the (combined) status-judgment variable upon associated values calculated to represent scores on factors I and II. For the Negro (T_n) and White teacher (T_w) data sets, the variance components representing factor I (confidence-eagerness), factor II (ethnicity-nonstandardness), and R^2 were:

$$R^2_{T_n} = (0.250) + (0.443) = 0.693$$

$$R^2_{T_w} = (0.364) + (0.540) = 0.904$$

Both of the foregoing coefficients indicated a relatively high degree of relation between the two factors and the status-judgments ($R_{T_n} = 0.832$; $R_{T_w} = 0.951$), although this relation was greater in the T_w as compared with the T_n data.[6] Additionally, these results indicated (as was expected from the factor loadings) that status-judgments were more related to factor II than to factor I, the former accounting for roughly 40% and the latter for about 60% of the predicted variance in both data sets.

Predictions of judgmental data from speech characteristics. Reflecting upon the "linkage" concept referred to earlier—i.e., the relation between speech characteristics and judgments about speakers—it was hypothesized that if individual speech characteristics are cues to a person's social status, then a set of such cues in quantified form should serve as salient predictor variables for the

---

[6]These two regression equations are intended as nothing more than a convenient description of the relation between the status ratings and the two dimensions of the judgmental model. Scores representative of the factors were based on the distribution of values created by the weighted (by factor loadings) combination of individual scale data for a factor, the combined score being standardized. In this phase the response data provided by different teachers for each stimulus tape were collapsed into separate mean ratings across White (T_w) and across Negro (T_n) teachers.

prediction of the status-judgments in the present data. Moreover, if the present interpretations regarding the two-factor judgmental model were valid, then the predictor variables for status-judgments should also relate in an interpretable fashion to the dimensions of the model. The first task was the collection and eventually the reduction of a set of predictor variables.

In the course of the previous research (Williams and Naremore, 1969a, b) involving these language samples, a great variety of detailed characteristics had been identified and quantified for each tape. Added to these were a set of further variables suggested from the results of the main study by Shuy, *et al.* (1967). Although space limitations prevent the detailed definitions of all the variables initially surveyed as potential predictors, they can be summarized as follows:

1. Production phenomena: This represents rate (syllables per sec.), and four types of hestitations—silent pauses, filled pauses, repeats, and false starts—as defined in the work of Maclay and Osgood (1959).

2. Amounts of production: This represents word count means for a child's total speech on a given topic, for his segments in the interaction, and a mean relative to the incidence of clause terminals (i.e., $\#$), counts of the number of times (speech segments) the child spoke in the interaction, and the number of clause terminals per segment.

3. Syntactic elaboration: Based upon measures reported by Williams and Naremore (1969b), these were the type and frequency of specified immediate constituent (syntactic) divisions in the different phrase environments of sentences and the relative frequency of clause fragments.

4. Functional characteristics: As reported in Williams and Naremore (1969a), these reflected the coding of the types of field workers' probes (whether they required the child to elaborate, etc.), the types of responses given by the child, grammatical perspective (use of first person, third person, etc.), and an index of the organization observed among a child's syntactic segments.

5. Nonstandard characteristics: Since the study by Shuy, *et al.* (1967) had reported detailed evidence on selected nonstandard linguistic characteristics, those characteristics with the most substantial variation by social status were further coded and quantified for use in this project. In brief, these included the incidence of deviation in verb constructions, pronominal apposition, variants in word-final [-s] and [-z], [-t] and [-d] and [-ŋ] sounds, and variants in medial and final [n], [m], [Θ], and [ð] sounds.

Initially there were 82 individual measures available for each language sample. As would be expected, not all of these were correlated with the status-judgments, and among those that were, many were redundant. The reduction of this list of variables was done with an eye toward developing relatively descriptive and interpretable (but not necessarily parsimonious)[7] linear equations for the prediction of the status-judgments. The first reduction omitted all variables which did not have zero-order correlations of at least 0.22 (significant at $p < 0.05$ with $df = 78$) with the status-judgment variable in either data set (T_n, T_w). The second reduction involved omitting or combining predictor variables, where such reductions could meet statistical criteria (e.g., high intercorrelation) as well as linguistic criteria (e.g., combination of items of similar grammatical types, as the counts of [-s] deviations in different word environments). The final stage of reduction was based on the successive modifications of predictors in stepwise regression analyses, again making omissions and combinations of predictors.[8] Eventually, the variables listed in Table 3.3 were those selected for the regression equations for the T_n and T_w data, and where status-judgment was the dependent variable. One additional variable, a binary coding of the child's race (1 = Negro, 2 = White), was incorporated into the analyses as a basis for describing this potential aspect of bias in the prediction equation. Table 3.4 presents the partial correlations between each predictor variable and status-judgments, based on the equations developed for the T_n and T_w data. Also included in Table 3.4 are partial correlations derived from separate regression equations calculated for factors I and II as dependent variables in the two data sets.

Interpretations. A first point was that both regression equations of status-judgment on the predictor variables, even with 18 predictors, yielded significant and relatively substantial multiple correlations ($p < 0.01$, $df = 18/61$). In brief, then, the amount of status-judgment variance accounted for in these regressions (about 40%) was thought to be sufficient to warrant more detailed interpretations of the equations. As for maximizing predicted variance (at the expense of descriptive goals), an earlier equation in the stepwise procedure for each data set yielded corrected multiple correlations greater than those given here.

The most general picture emerging in Table 3.4 was that selected variables among the 18 could be identified as salient predictors of the status-judgments, and in many instances each of these could further be identified with a dimension

---

[7] Here, "parsimonious" refers to an equation with fewer predictor variables. We were more interested in predictor variable patterns than in minimizing predictors and the "cost" of degrees of freedom in interpreting the significance of R^2 (Guilford, 1956, pp. 398-399).

[8] "Stepwise" analyses refer to a procedure in which a regression equation is calculated using first as a predictor that variable with the highest zero-order correlation with the dependent variable. A next equation involves the incorporation of the predictor variable leading to the greatest increase in R^2 in a two-predictor equation, then incorporation of a third predictor, and so on. See Darlington (1968) for further details, criteria for interpretation, etc.

TABLE 3.3

*Variables Incorporated as Predictors in the Final
Regression Equations*

Label	Description

Production Phenomena

1. *Silent pauses:* frequency of silences judged of "unusual length" (cf. Maclay and Osgood, 1959), divided by the number of words spoken by the child.

2. *Filled pauses:* frequency of vocalized hesitation devices (mainly [ə]), divided by the number of words spoken by the child (Maclay and Osgood, 1959).

Amounts of Production

3. *Juncture total:* number of clause terminals (mainly #) in the child's responses on a topic (Williams and Naremore, 1969a).

4. *Word total:* number of words spoken by a child on a topic.

Syntactic Elaboration

5. *Clause fragments:* relative frequency of syntactic units not classifiable as clauses.

6. *Sentence length:* mean number of immediate constituent divisions per sentence.

7. *Verb construction:* mean number of immediate constituent division in verb constructions.

Functional Characteristics

8. *Reticence index:* relative frequency of instances where the field worker's probes for elaboration were not followed by elaboration in the child's responses.

9. *Introductory interjections:* frequency of words such as *now, anyhow, well,* and *oh* which typically appeared at the beginning of a child's responses.

TABLE 3.3 (continued)

Nonstandard Characteristics

10. *Pronominal apposition:* as in, "The other guy, *he* came. . . ."; frequency of such pronoun usage (cf. Shuy, *et al.,* 1967, pp. 23 *ff.*).

11. *Deviations in main verb:* relative frequency of any deviation in the verb construction, except those involving the phenomena listed below.

12. *[-s] or [-z] deviations:* final position: relative frequency in first ten occurrences of the item.

13. *[Θ] or [ð] deviations:* medial (ten occurrences) and final (ten occurrences) data combined.

14. *[-t] or [-d] deviations:* final position.

15. *[m] deviations:* medial and final positions combined.

16. *[n] deviations:* medial and final positions combined.

17. *[ŋ] deviations:* final position.

TABLE 3.4

Partial Correlations of Predictor Variables Obtained from Regression Equations Where Status-Judgments and Factor Scores Were Dependent Variables

Variables	Negro Teachers			White Teachers		
		Factors			Factors	
	Status-Judg.	I	II	Status-Judg.	I	II
Silent pauses	-0.38†*	-0.40*	-0.05	-0.26†*	-0.36*	-0.13
Filled pauses	0.11	0.10	-0.02	0.06	0.02	0.01
Juncture total	0.26†*	0.21	0.11	0.09	0.15	-0.08
Word total	-0.11	-0.09	0.01	0.01	0.07	0.20
Clause fragments	-0.22†	0.19	-0.16	-0.09	0.16	-0.31*
Sentence length	0.09	0.00	0.16	0.29†*	0.13	-0.28*
Verb construction	0.15	0.11	0.13	0.33†*	0.15	0.29*

TABLE 3.4 (continued)

Reticence index	-0.30†*	-0.18	-0.11	-0.07	0.04	-0.05
Introductory interj.	0.11	0.03	0.09	0.15†	0.04	0.12
Pronominal apposition	-0.30†*	-0.05	-0.22	-0.22†	-0.19	-0.33*
Deviations in main verb	-0.21†	-0.23	-0.16	-0.23†	-0.22*	-0.25*
[-s] or [-z] deviations	-0.08	0.07	-0.32*	-0.17†	0.14	-0.40*
[Θ] or [ð] deviations	-0.27†*	-0.16	-0.34*	-0.29†*	-0.02	-0.39*
[-t] or [-d] deviations	-0.17†	0.03	-0.03	0.12†	0.05	0.00
[m] deviations	-0.06	-0.13	-0.15	0.08	-0.04	-0.24
[n] deviations	0.04	-0.05	-0.10	-0.08	0.01	-0.15
[ŋ] deviations	0.06	0.22	-0.02	0.00	0.07	-0.03
Child's race	-0.03	0.26*	-0.23	-0.22†	0.05	-0.41*
(R corrected, 18 variables)	(0.63)	(0.58)	(0.66)	(0.63)	(0.44)	(0.81)

†Variables included in the regression equation having the highest corrected R.

*Regression coefficient significantly ($p < 0.05$) different from zero in 18-predictor equations.

in the judgmental model. Thus, for example, the incidence of silent pausing was related to status-judgments in both data sets; moreover, it showed an interpretable greater relation with the confidence-eagerness factor (I) than with ethnicity-nonstandardness (II). By contrast, the incidence of pronominal apposition was related to status-judgments, but, as might be expected, it correlated with ethnicity-nonstandardness more so than with confidence-eagerness. Deviations in voiced and voiceless *th* sounds had a similar correlational pattern. Some other such interpretable patterns (and a few paradoxical ones) can be seen in the T_w and T_n arrays. Taken as an overall picture, most of the results shown in Table 3.4 are evidence of the integrity of the two-factor judgmental model, at least insofar as it could be related to the characteristics of the language sample. A final note on the array was that the child's race, included to determine the bias of this variable in the equation, did show a salient relation with status-judgments in the White teachers' ratings but not in data from the Negro teachers. Although the child's race was related to the factor scores in the Negro teachers' ratings, it was independent of their status-judgments.

A note of caution: The low partial correlations in Table 3.4 did not necessarily mean that a variable was unrelated to status-judgments (recall that all had a significant zero-order correlation in either the T_n or T_w data), but that other variables, being more related to the dependent variables, lessened the magnitude of their partial correlation.

Judged status as against actual status. An obvious question was how accurately the teachers had judged the actual characteristics of the children. Here the question was focused on how status-judgments differed according to the child's actual status (as defined in the language sample), and how this difference, in turn, varied according to the child's race, sex, speech topic, and the race of the teacher-listener. An analysis of variance was conducted in which status-judgments served as the dependent variable, and the individual children as replicates, and where response data were partitioned by teacher race, the speech topic, and the children's status, race, and sex. Results were interpreted with an eye toward expected differences on the status dimension and for possible interactions with this difference.

As anticipated, the mean ratings assigned to the high status group (12.9) exceeded those assigned to the lower group (10.2: $F = 16.1, df = 1/32, p < 0.01$). There was, however, one significant ($F = 7.3, df = 1/32, p < 0.05$) three-way interaction involving the status dimension; this was child race × child sex × status. Here, multiple mean comparisons (Duncan, 1955) revealed that although significant ($p < 0.05$) status differences prevailed in the status comparisons of Negro male children (H. S. = 11.3, L. S. = 7.6) and Negro females (H. S. = 14.5, L. S. = 7.5), the status difference was short of statistical significance at this level for male White children (H. S. = 12.3, L. S. = 11.1; $p < 0.15$), and was opposite from expectations for White females (H. S. = 13.5, L. S. = 14.8; $p < 0.13$). In short, then, it could be said that reliable status differentiations were made for Negro children, although by negative implication the lack of further significant interactions was evidence of the generality of such differentiations across the further parameters of teacher race and speech topic.

Discussion

The overall results of the study may be summarized as follows:

1. The general judgmental model appeared to incorporate two factors—a differentiation of children in terms of their overall participation in the interview, generally labeled as confidence-eagerness, and a differentiation presumably

reflective of the type of language employed by the child, generally labeled as ethnicity-nonstandardness.

2. Ratings of a child's social status could largely be accounted for within the two-factor model. Presumably "sounding disadvantaged" or "low class" would be associated with perceiving a child as reticent or unsure in the speech situation, but even more so with his sounding ethnic and nonstandard in his language usage.

3. For the present language samples, ratings of status as well as the judgmental dimensions could be reliably predicted on the basis of selected features of speech and language found in the samples. Among the most salient predictors were the incidence of silent pausing (inversely related to ratings of confidence-eagerness) and deviations from standard English such as pronominal apposition, main verb construction, and the articulation of selected phonemes (related to ethnicity-nonstandardness).

4. Statistically reliable judged differentiations of a child's actual social status were found mainly in the case of Negro male and female children rather than White children.

Although the two-factor model was clearly suggested in the factor analytic results and was further supported in the prediction equations, there was nevertheless evidence of variations thought mainly reflective of the factors of teacher race and child race. At least such factors were of more consequence in the rating data than were the speech topic or sex of the child.

One distinction across teacher race was that ratings of a child's race were more of a central correlate of factor II (ethnicity-nonstandardness) for White teachers than for Negro teachers. The initial evidence of this distinction was the different correlations of the race scale (17) on factor II: -0.86 for White teachers, -0.69 for Negroes. Moreover, White teachers' ratings of race were more correlated with status-judgments (-0.55) than were those of Negro teachers (-0.27). Even the influence of the child's actual race appeared greater in the White teachers' ratings than in those of their Negro counterparts. The binary coding of child race loomed as a significant predictor variable in status-judgment equations calculated for White teachers but not in those for Negro teachers (cf. Table 3.4).

Although the foregoing differences did not seem to affect significantly overall status differentiations (as indicated by the lack of interactions involving teacher and child race in the analysis of variance results), they did reflect differences in the bases for such differentiations. These differences could be seen in the distributions of children as gained by dichotomizing the data on the status-judgment and race scales. White teachers, for example, placed 17 of the 20 White children in the upper half of the status distribution, as against only 12 White children so rated by the Negro teachers. All White children, whether rated high or low in status, or by Negro or White teachers, were rated as being White. As for Negro children, nine (of 20) were located in the high category by White teachers, but six of these children were also rated as being White (all, incidentally, were from the original H. S. sample). Of the eight Negro children placed in the high category by Negro teachers, only two were rated on the White half of the race scale, and only barely so in terms of the magnitude of the ratings. In short, the bias in the White teachers' ratings might be summarized as: sounding White is equated with high status.

Little more than a warning need be given concerning the fact that the present model was based upon the intersection of highly specific populations (the children, the teachers, the speech topic, etc.), and this, of course, may place major restrictions on the generality of the model and the results of its application beyond the kinds of situations represented in the present samples.[9]

Although the factor analytic results pointed to a two-factor model, it must be remembered that this model was developed at considerable expense to our knowledge of individual teacher differences in judgmental behavior (which, save for race, were subsumed in the early analyses). In the course of the analyses there was the observation, for example, that in terms of scale values, teachers were usually more consistent with themselves in differentiating, say, high status children from lower status ones, than they were with other teachers' ratings of the same children. Although this observation is the subject of the Naremore study, it does give evidence of stereotyping in the individual teacher's judgmental behavior. That is, as was found by Lambert et al. (1960), the speech cues may elicit some type of general personality, cultural, or ethnic stereotype, and most of a teacher's judgments draw from this stereotype rather than from the continuous and detailed variety of input cues. That a teacher will readily develop a detailed set of expectations about a child, even when such expectations are contrived (Rosenthal and Jacobson, 1968), is evidence that such stereotypes exist and are part of the dynamics of teacher-pupil behaviors.

If substantial evidence of stereotyping were found, it would probably not loom as a counterargument to the present interpretations; rather, it should augment them. What the present results represent is a type of collective picture generated for teachers as groups rather than as individuals. Knowledge about individual teacher's judgments, or how teachers might be grouped on the basis of

---

[9]Two further studies using this data are reported in this monograph. One, immediately following this section, involves a factoring of the teachers rather than the scales, thus telling us something of the generality of the present model on a teacher-by-teacher basis. The second study involved gathering response data to the same tapes but using teachers from a southern school. These results are reported in Chapter 6 of this monograph and in a paper by Frederick Williams and Wayne Shamo (Purdue University, 1972).

such judgments, could add to the explanation of what might lie between the detailed types of behavior in individual teachers and the dimensions of the proposed model.

To conclude with a practical implication: although both groups of teachers were relatively similar in terms of the results of status-judgments, it has been pointed out that White teachers' status-judgments seemed to reflect a more direct association between race and status, both in terms of judged race and the child's actual race. Rather than evidence of some type of purposive bias on the part of the White teachers, this may be a reflection of a stereotype of pupil language which more strongly equates standardness with linguistic effectiveness and social status than would be found with the Negro teachers. It could probably be assumed that most of the Negro teachers, through the language experiences of their childhood coupled with the language of their educational programs, had developed a sensitivity to Negro and White styles of speech and were more able than their White counterparts to differentiate levels of effectiveness and status in both styles. By contrast, the White teachers' experience with Negro speech has presumably been mostly confined to the schoolroom, where standardness is a key criterion. It is not unusual, then, that they exhibited judgmental behavior more tied to a child's actual race, and to perceptions of race, in their status evaluations of speech and language.

The Naremore Study of Teacher Differences[10]

Emerging from the Chicago analyses was the generalization that teachers would provide reliable but rather gross evaluations of the children's speech samples. In investigating the characteristics of this unexpected gross quality in the ratings, it was found that the individual teachers themselves tended to have substantial differences in their actual ratings of the children. Thus while an overall analysis divided only by teacher race revealed a general picture of a gross two-dimensional judgmental model, there remained the key problem of investigating and hopefully interpreting individual teacher differences in the response data.

Problem

The specific aim of the present phase of the investigation was to ferret out a picture of the individual teacher differences. Stated in question form, the problem was: (1) *to what extent could the teachers be grouped together in terms*

---

[10]Except for introductory and transition sections and minor editing, this section is essentially a reprinting of the article "Teachers' Judgments of Children's Speech: A Factor Analytic Study of Attitudes" by Rita C. Naremore, published in *Speech Monographs,* March, 1971, *38,* pp. 17-27.

of commonality in their attitudinal responses? Put another way, this question asks whether underlying the gross picture provided in the earlier analysis there might be a more detailed and accurate picture of specific types of teachers as defined by the commonality of their rating behavior. Additionally, if groups of teachers could be isolated or defined, (2) *to what extent could they be contrasted and compared in terms of teacher characteristics, child characteristics, rating scale characteristics, and selected characteristics of the speech samples themselves?*

The data from the Chicago study were used for analysis here. For an account of the methodology and for a description of the semantic differential scales, see the previous section of this chapter.

Analysis and Interpretations

In overview, the general research strategy was to attempt to group the teachers, using factor analytic techniques, on the basis of their responses to the children's speech samples. The teacher types or groups arising from this factor analysis were compared and contrasted in terms of the ratings given to the different types of children on the semantic differential scales. In order to complete the picture of the teachers' behavior, a correlation analysis was undertaken to investigate the correlates of their judgmental behavior in the speech of the children.

The factor analysis. The factor analysis was accomplished by use of a form of inverted matrix factor analysis, related to Stephenson's Q-analysis. The analysis yielded four factors, which are shown in Table 3.5. This table contains a listing of the teachers by identification number, arranged according to the types, or factors, into which the teachers can be divided. The letter to the right of each teacher identification denotes the race of that teacher. The loading of each teacher on each factor is presented in the four columns headed I-IV. Thus in reading the table, it can be seen that teacher number 26, who is White, is a part of factor I. Her loading on the factor is .717. As Table 3.5 shows, the four factors are bipolar, and the bipolarity is closely related to teacher race, except in the first factor, where all the teachers are White.

Before proceeding further with the discussion of the factor analysis, two cautions are in order. First, it should be noted that among the teachers who make up any given factor, there appear to be differences in the degree of their "belonging" to the factor. For example, teacher 26 is clearly a part of factor I, as her loading here is substantial and also much higher than her loading on any other factor. Teacher 10, however, has a very low loading on factor I, as she does on all factors. It might be said that she is not really a substantial part of any factor. Teacher 9, on the other hand, has a reasonably high loading on factor I,

TABLE 3.5

Variable Loadings by Factor

Factor:	I	II	III	IV
FACTOR I–9 White				
teachers				
26W	-0.717	0.192	-0.003	-0.039
25W	- .684	.195	.023	.169
24W	- .619	.018	.147	.190
27W	- .663	- .099	.104	- .264
10W	.248	- .113	- .025	.134
23W	- .574	- .032	.266	- .451
12W	.497	.157	.398	- .355
6W	.487	.391	- .068	- .402
9W	.483	.361	.410	- .258
FACTOR II–5 Negro, 5				
White teachers				
17W	- .004	- .514	- .106	.040
2W	.171	.707	.013	- .002
11N	.179	- .480	- .051	.022
4N	.103	- .604	.112	- .200
5W	.071	.573	- .264	- .002
7N	.295	- .605	- .060	- .246
3W	.092	.526	- .046	- .328
1N	.302	- .520	.091	- .193
20W	.148	- .251	.076	.237
16N	- .118	- .132	- .103	- .102
FACTOR III–2 Negro,				
5 White teachers				
30W	0.160	-0.006	-0.758	-0.106
29W	.263	- .071	- .664	- .032
32N	.071	.184	- .568	.152
13W	.223	.274	.416	.068
22W	- .296	- .038	.347	.141
33N	- .361	.208	- .438	.294
14W	.432	.246	.474	.332
8W	.165	.464	.466	.437

TABLE 3.5 (continued)

Factor:	I	II	III	IV
FACTOR IV–4 Negro, 2 White teachers				
21W	- .040	.039	.101	.489
19N	.061	- .090	.119	.590
15N	.068	- .041	.084	- .270
31W	.080	.165	- .194	.545
18N	- .290	- .196	.079	.538
28N	- .134	- .353	.009	- .403
TOTAL				
VAR.–PER FACTOR	.1186	.1128	.0879	.0873
–CUMULATIVE	.1186	.2314	.3193	.4066
COM. VAR–PER FACTOR	.2916	.2774	.2163	.2147
–CUMULATIVE	.2916	.5691	.7853	1.0000

but loads almost as high on factor III. It might be said that she is almost as much like the type 3 teachers as she is like the type 1 teachers. Although these teachers and others like them could have been eliminated from the analysis, they were not, because a weighting procedure in the computer program assured that no entire teacher type would be described in terms of the behavior of these factorally complex teachers. However, because the complexity does exist, it will be well to bear in mind the following: The remarks which will be made here concerning the behavior of any teacher type cannot and should not be taken as descriptions of teachers as a whole, or of any individual teacher. The teacher types discussed in this study are, to that extent, abstractions. The second word of caution relates to the discussion of teacher race in the study. As a brief examination of Table 3.5 shows, the teacher types are divided roughly along lines of teacher race, but it should be noted that all the types except type 1 are racially mixed. Thus the use of the qualifier "roughly."

With these cautions in mind, we can now examine more closely the results of the factor analysis. It is evident that the first major question of the study—can teachers be grouped on the basis of their rating behavior?—can be answered in the affirmative. That is, the teachers' responses were neither totally idiosyncratic, as would have been indicated by a large number of factors, each composed of one or two teachers; nor were the responses totally global, as would have been indicated had most of the teachers fallen into one large factor. We can, then, turn to the second question—to what extent can the types of teachers found be compared and contrasted in terms of teacher characteristics, child characteristics, rating scale characteristics, and characteristics of the speech samples themselves? The factor analysis program employed in the study provided a breakdown of the rating behavior of each teacher type, which makes the answers to this question readily available.

First, how do the types differ in terms of the teachers found in each type? Although the teachers in the study differed in terms of their degree of teaching experience, their length of time spent in inner city schools, the type of training they had, and such other factors as sex, religion, and marital status, the one teacher characteristic which served to differentiate the types in any way was teacher race. For type 1, the teachers are all White, and in the other types, the bipolarity of the factor tends to split the type along lines of teacher race. As Table 3.5 shows, type 2 was split with the positive loading segment being all White and the negative segment being predominantly Black—only two White teachers were in this negative segment. Examination of the backgrounds of the teachers found in this type revealed that the two White teachers grouped in the negative segment with the five Black teachers were the only two White teachers in the sample who indicated having had experiences with inner city children outside the school. Regrettably, no such explanation exists for the racial mix in any of the other type splits. Type 3, for example, has four White teachers loading positively and three Black teachers and one White teacher loading negatively. There does not appear to be anything in the information available about that one White teacher which would explain why she behaved like those three Black teachers. The same applies to the teachers in type 4.

A second area of type contrast is that of teachers' ratings of different types of children on the semantic differential scales. The only scale which stood out in type contrasts was the pronunciation standardness scale, which served to differentiate between the positive and negative loading segments of each type. That is, where the positive loading segment of a type tended to rate most children low on this scale, the negative loading segment would tend to rate them high, or vice versa. The various types of teachers also differed in the accuracy of their judgments on the scales—that is, in the degree to which these judgments conform to objective measures of the children's performance. The most accurate ratings of the child types were those of type 2 teachers, both segments of which rated high status children of both races across the scales. This behavior is in agreement with results of previous analyses by Williams and Naremore (1969a, b) which indicated that the high status children generally exceeded the performance of low status children on both syntactic and functional measures of language. In no case did any group of Black teachers consistently rate children of their own race above White children, although two segments of White teachers (the positive segments of types 1 and 3) exhibited this kind of racial bias in rating White children above Black children. Additionally, there was a type of teacher whose behavior could be labeled "overcompensation" in the sense that she rated children whose performance was actually low (low status children) above children whose performance was actually high (high status children). This behavior was exhibited by the negative loading segments of types 1 and 3 and the positive loading segment of type 4. Teachers in the negative segment of type 4 tended ro rate girls higher than boys across the scales, and this was the only instance of a sex contrast in the ratings.

Interpretations. Perhaps the most striking aspect of the results of this first phase of analysis is the influence of the race of the teacher on her ratings of the children. There are a number of reasons for expecting race to influence the subjective responses a teacher might have to children's language. Most Black teachers have undoubtedly had more contact with, and even more experience with, standard English than most White teachers have had with Black speech patterns. One would expect the Black teachers, then, to be more sensitive to the details of the speech of both White and Black children, and the White teachers to respond to the speech of the Black children on a fairly gross level, not being sensitive to the subtle details of the dialect. It is also likely that Black teachers might be more willing to recognize a Black child as high status than the White teachers in this study. Since the White teachers are likely to have had most of their contacts with Black speech in the schools, and since these teachers work in inner city, often economically deprived, school areas they are likely to associate sounding Black with sounding low status. The Black teachers, in contrast, are more likely to have had experience with middle-class Blacks and are not so likely to associate race and social status in this way.

The correlation analysis. In order to examine the final area of contrast among the teacher types—that of differences in the objective correlates of the subjective ratings assigned by the teacher types—a correlation analysis was performed. The objective variables used in the correlation analysis were obtained from previous analyses of the data by Williams and Naremore (1969a, b) and from the Chicago study. The variables included in the analysis are presented in Table 3.6. The correlation analysis was performed separately for each teacher type. The scores for each of the 16 types of children for each of the 18 measures shown in Table 3.7 were correlated with the subjective ratings given to the 16 types of children on the 12 semantic differential scales by each teacher in a type.

One question of major interest in this analysis was how well the two-factor model found in previous analyses would hold up. The answer to this question can be seen in Table 3.7, which shows, for each teacher type, the three highest correlations between ratings on the family status and pronunciation standardness

TABLE 3.6
Objective Variables Used in the Correlation Analyses

Production phenomena

1. Silent pauses—frequency of silences judged of "unusual length" divided by the number of words spoken by the child.

2. Filled pauses—frequency of vocalized hesitation devices (such as "uh" and "ah") divided by the total number of words spoken by the child.

Amounts of production

3. Juncture total—number of clause terminals (linguistically, double cross junctures) per topic in the child's speech.

4. Word total—number of words on a given topic.

Syntactic elaboration

5. Clause fragments—relative frequency of syntactic fragments (not classifiable as clauses).

6. Sentence length—mean number of immediate constituent divisions per sentence.

7. Verb construction—mean number of immediate constituent divisions in verb constructions.

Functional characteristics

8. Reticence index—relative frequency of instances where the field worker asked for a simple yes-no response and the child gave an elaborated response.

9. Introductory interjections—frequency of words such as "well," "now," and "oh" which appeared at the beginning of a child's utterance.

10. Organization—degree of relatedness among the units of the child's utterance.

scales and objective characteristics of the children's speech. As this table indicates, pronunciation deviations and pausal phenomena in the child's speech are salient correlates of these ratings for all the teacher types. This finding bears out the earlier interpretation that the teachers responded to the children's

TABLE 3.6 (continued)

Nonstandard characteristics

11. Pronominal apposition—frequency of.

12. Deviations in main verb—frequency of deviations (except phonological) in verb construction.

13. [s] or [z] deviations—final position; relative frequency in first ten occurrences of the item.

14. [θ] or [ð] deviations—medial (ten occurrences) and final (ten occurrences) data combined.

15. [t] or [d] deviations—final position.

16. [m] deviations—medial and final positions combined.

17. [n] deviations—medial and final positions combined.

18. [ŋ] deviations—final position

---

speech in terms of the two gross dimensions of nonstandardness-ethnicity and confidence-eagerness. The most salient objective measures found in the correlation analysis are directly related to those two gross dimensions of judgment. The subjective-objective correlations involving pronunciation deviations and pausal phenomena appear also to be fairly undifferentiated. That is, there are no clear-cut correlations of pronunciation scale or pausal variables with the confidence scale. Rather, it is more the case that every scale correlates significantly with most of these variables across the four teacher types.

Beyond this commonality of response to pausal and pronunciation variables, the teacher types do differ in terms of the saliency of other types of variables. The predominantly White teacher types (1 and 3) have high correlations between their judgments and such qualitative variables as verb constructions, while the predominantly Black teacher types (2 and 4) have high correlations between their judgments and such quantitative variables as total words in the message.

Interpretation. The difference in the degree of correlation of these latter variables suggests that there is one kind of teacher who is concerned primarily with details in a child's speech. She might be characterized as being a kind of "detail oriented rater." On the other hand, there is a kind of teacher who is able to apprehend the totality of a child's performance—his willingness to participate in an interview situation, and his ability to become involved in a topic to the extent of having a great deal to say about it. This kind of teacher

TABLE 3.7
*Three Highest Correlations Between Objective Variables
and Pronunciation Standardness and
Family Status Scales*

	Type I Teachers		
	Pronunciation Standardness		Family Status
s, z Deviations	-.448	Θ Deviations	-.429
Main Verb Deviations	-.447	Verb Constructions	.363
Silent Pauses	-.444	Main Verb Deviations	-.338
	Type II Teachers		
t, d Deviations	-.486	t, d Deviations	- .434
Silent Pauses	-.486	Silent Pauses	-.429
s, z Deviations	-.466	Intro. Interjections	.417
	Type III Teachers		
Filled Pauses	-.454	Θ Deviations	- .564
Silent Pauses	-.436	Filled Pauses	-.471
t, d Deviations	-.428	t, d Deviations	-.457
	Type IV Teachers		
s, z Deviations	-.562	Silent Pauses	-.411
Main Verb Deviations	-.519	s, z Deviations	-.395
Silent Pauses	-.505	t, d Deviations	-.366

might be characterized as a "communication oriented rater." The question arises here as to why the White teachers seemed more likely to be the detail oriented raters. One can only speculate, but it could be related to the fact that so much of language education in the American school system is of a prescriptionist nature. That is, what the child is taught in school is that there is a right way to use language, and this right way consists of using certain details of syntax and vocabulary in prescribed ways. The point at which the White and Black teachers differ here is that the White teachers have never encountered another language system which was of any importance to them, which contained its own set of expectations for the right way to talk. That is, the White teachers, by virtue of being essentially monolingual, have always found their linguistic standards applicable. The Black teachers, on the other hand, are of necessity bicultural and bilingual, and so probably discovered long ago that the prescriptionist rules of good standard English did not apply in many situations they encountered. Hence, they are more likely than White teachers to have dropped these rules for use of language details as viable bases for judgment of people.

Discussion

The conclusions arising from the results of this study can be summarized by reference to the two questions which the study was designed to answer.

1. To what extent can teachers be grouped together in terms of the commonality of their attitudinal responses to children's speech? The present analysis yielded four types of teachers, differing from one another in various dimensions of judgment.

2. To what extent can groups of teachers be contrasted and compared in terms of teacher characteristics, child characteristics, rating scale characteristics, and selected characteristics of the children's speech? Three conclusions of the present study relate to this question. First, the teacher types found in this study were divided, both between and within types, roughly along lines of teacher race. Second, the teacher types differed in kinds of judgments they made and in the accuracy of those judgments across different kinds of children and different semantic differential scales. Third, pronunciation deviations and pausal phenomena were correlates of the subjective ratings for all teacher types, but teacher types differed, roughly along lines of race in the correlations between subjective judgments and qualitative versus quantitative variables in the children's speech.

chapter 4

THE TEXAS RESEARCH

Introduction and Preliminaries

The results of the Chicago research led to a number of questions for further investigation, one of which was how teachers' attitudes toward different dialects might be related to expectancy of pupils' classroom performance. This question seemed particularly significant in view of the issues raised by Rosenthal and Jacobson in *Pygmalion in the Classroom* (1968).[1] Could dialect attitudes be associated with expectations of pupils' performance in particular subject matter areas? In designing research to answer this overall question several other factors were considered. Among these was the methodological assumption that videotapes as compared with audiotapes, would provide a closer approximation to the actual classroom stimulus situation for making generalizations about teachers' attitudinal behavior.[2] There was also the issue of whether the two-factor judgmental model of confidence-eagerness and ethnicity-nonstandardness would emerge with videotapes and with different populations of teachers and pupils. If the model were obtained, how would judgments vary as a function of teacher experience and ethnicity? A final question was the degree to which stereotyping could be said to play a role in teachers' evaluations of children's language. To what degree might a teacher simply report her

---

[1] The authors are well aware of the controversy surrounding this study; see, for example, Fleming and Anttonen (1971).

[2] This, of course, meant that teachers were no longer responding strictly to speech samples, but to dress, visual cues of ethnicity, and the like. The effects of the visual image with the use of an ethnic guise are the topics of another report (Williams, Whitehead, and Miller, 1971) and included in Chapter 6 of this monograph.

attitudinal predispositions in evaluating a child from a particular ethnic group, rather than carefully evaluating the details of what is presented for assessment?

The present investigation was designed to answer the foregoing questions based upon data from the field study in which teachers from schools selected within Central Texas evaluated videotape speech samples of Black, Anglo,[3] and Mexican-American children sampled from middle and low status homes. Although the emphasis in the main study was on Anglo and Black teachers, Miller (1972 and later in this chapter) undertook a detailed analysis of the Mexican-American teachers, comparing them with a matched group of Anglo teachers. After a description of the language samples and several necessary pilot studies, the first portion of the main Texas study is an account of ways in which teachers differentiated the children and how these differentiations were related to stereotypes in academic attitudes.[4]

The second half of this chapter focuses upon the differences that were found among the teachers by applying a Q-analysis similar to that used by Naremore in the Chicago research. Again, the Q-analysis was conducted to determine if ratings of the videotapes would indicate heterogeneity among the teachers' rating behaviors. Given evidence of different teacher rating types, teacher characteristics could be contrasted in terms of ethnicity, rating biases, and school characteristics. Generalizations about these teacher rating biases could then be evaluated.

The Language Samples

The key to the Texas research was that videotape samples be obtained of children in the three ethnic and two status groups described earlier. Several somewhat arbitrary decisions were necessary in obtaining these samples.

Child characteristics. Mainly for the purposes of being able to compare the present series of studies with the Chicago study, it was decided to sample speech from fifth- and sixth-grade children. For purposes of economy in the present project, and since no differences were observed in the ratings of males and females in the previous study, only boys were recorded.

Status was defined largely upon the basis of the child's neighborhood, which in all cases corresponded also to the location of his school. Ethnicity was identified by the researchers. Altogether, 41 children were contacted by liaison with schools in or near Austin, Texas. Of these, the ethnic and status

---

[3]These are common labels in Central Texas. The term "Anglo" as used here refers to Caucasian children who are not Mexican-American. Note also that we refer to "Black" rather than "Negro," which was more a reflection of changes in national attitudes as compared with the earlier Chicago research.

[4]For more details see Williams, *et al.,* 1971a, and 1972.

characteristics were: six Black, low; six Black, middle; six Anglo, low; seven Anglo, middle; nine Mexican-American, low; seven Mexican-American, middle.

The status identifications of the children's families can be additionally described in terms of the fathers' occupations. Representative occupations included:

	Low Status	Middle Status
Anglo	Laborer for Gas Company	Architect
Black	Laundry Worker	Professor of Sociology
Mexican- American	Service Station Employee	Painting Contractor

Speech style. Rather than sample different speech styles, it was decided to elicit the type of speech expected between child and teacher (presuming a relatively friendly teacher). In terms of contemporary studies of social dialects, this would be a semi-formal speech style. Questions asked of the child were the same as used in the free-speech portions of the Detroit Dialect Study (Shuy, Wolfram, and Riley, 1967):

(1) "What kinds of games do you play?"
(2) "What are some of your favorite TV programs?"

Given responses to these opening questions, the child was encouraged to engage in free conversation (e.g., "How do you play baseball?" "What happened on Gunsmoke?").

Circumstances of the interview. Permission was sought from families to interview the children on weekends, holidays, or after school in a livingroom-like atmosphere arranged in facilities of the Center for Communication Research on The University of Texas at Austin campus. The children were transported to the campus in small groups ranging from three to six at a time, and were usually from the same ethnic and status groups. Prior to individual interviews, the children were entertained in a small conference room by being given plastic car models to assemble and provided with snacks of various kinds. At most times, a college undergraduate student of the same ethnic group as the children supervised the groups. Children were interviewed individually in the room mentioned earlier. Each child was seated on a bench near the interviewer's upright chair. The interviewer, an Anglo female in her mid-twenties, immediately struck up a casual conversation by asking the child about his family. Usually within several minutes, the atmosphere was sufficiently relaxed so that the interviewer could proceed with the scheduled questions. Each child was engaged in approximately eight minutes of conversation, all of which was videotaped.

Videotape recordings were done on an Ampex 6000 recorder using an Electro-Voice 644 dynamic microphone. These recordings comprised the master files of the project.

Tape editing. For the studies described in the subsequent sections of this chapter, segments were selected from the master file of videotapes. Segments were typically taken from selections on the master tapes at similar points in the interview, such as of children responding to the same question. Edited segments were dubbed from the master tapes first to a tape on another Ampex 6000 recorder and then to a one-half inch test tape using a Sony AV 3600 recorder. The Ampex 6000 recorder was employed in the pilot studies. Because portability was needed in the main project, the Sony AV 3600 was used.

Pilot Studies

In the process of preparing for the main Texas study, three preliminary studies were undertaken. The first of these was to develop the scaling instrument, and this followed the same lines as was used in the Chicago research. The second study, mainly for methodological purposes, was an investigation of the lengths of time that listeners needed in order to listen to tapes and to fill in appropriate scales. Finally, the third study was an attempt to see the degree to which teacher-subjects would respond to *labels* of children from different ethnic groups and social status when filling out the semantic differential scales. The latter types of ratings were based on a teacher's "experience" with children of a certain type and her "anticipations" as to how they would act. As such, they were regarded as an index of teacher's *stereotypes*. Since these studies contained greater detail than is pertinent to the aim of this monograph, and because this information is available elsewhere (Williams, Whitehead, and Miller, 1971), only their aims and general results will be summarized.

Semantic differential development. The first question of the Texas research was whether the semantic differential could be developed along the lines of the approach used in the Chicago study. Of the several differences in the Texas research, one was that audiovisual stimuli rather than audio recordings could be used. Another was that in addition to Anglo and Black children, Mexican-American children would be included. Finally, there is a more general question of whether the kinds of judgmental factors found in Chicago would be found again. This pilot study essentially involved presenting the segments of the video stimulus tapes to different groups of teachers, gathering adjectives from their descriptions of the tapes, then developing prototype scaling instruments.

The prototype instruments were subsequently used in a larger data gathering phase, and a final test instrument was obtained. This instrument was very much like the one used in the Chicago research, in that it reflected the two main factors of evaluation—namely, confidence-eagerness and ethnicity-nonstandardness. The differences from the Chicago study were in some of the detailed adjectives. (The reader is invited to compare the scales listed in subsequent tables of this chapter with those in the previous one.) In all, arguments were developed for the validity and the reliability of the Texas semantic differential estimate. Validity was assessed by the degree to which the scales would differentiate children who had been originally selected upon the basis of contrasts in language features, social status, and the like. Reliability was obtained from the pilot study data by the method of intraclass correlation. Essentially, this latter is a statistical index of the degree to which similar scales predict one another.

Another facet of this pilot study was the degree to which the rating instrument would be used similarly when stimuli were in an audio only, video only, and audiovisual mode of presentation. For the most part, the two-factor model was relevant to all three such modes. However, there was some evidence of a modality scale interaction, and details on this can be found in the aforementioned report. The importance for the present purposes was the finding that the two-factor model would apply to the audiovisual stimulus materials to be used in the main Texas study, and that the measurements would give us some confidence of being valid and reliable.

Judgmental response time. One practical question in the studies of the present type is the amount of stimulus material that a person needs in order to make his judgments. Although there has been research which has investigated the degree to which people will make judgments based upon briefer and briefer amounts of exposure to stimulus, there has not been more than an informal study of the amount of exposure that might be considered most "comfortable" or "adequate" to a listener. Secondly, there is a more theoretically oriented question of whether responses on one of the judgmental dimensions might substantially precede those of the other. For example, it was reasoned that the cues relevant to ethnicity-nonstandardness usually appear so frequently on a tape, that judgments on this dimension might be made before judgments of confidence-eagerness. Accordingly, it was reasonable to expect that perhaps judgments on one dimension might confound judgments on the other.

Essentially, this study involved the presentation of videotape stimulus materials to listeners, but under conditions where the listener could control operation of the tape presentation. Further, instead of filling out semantic differential scales as printed on a sheet, each scale was on a separate IBM card, and the cards were distributed in a random order on the desks in front of the listener. Such a procedure allowed for the measurement of: (1) the amount of time that the listener would run the stimulus tapes, (2) the order in which he would choose to fill out the scales, and (3) the average amount of stimulus exposure relative to the filling out of each of the semantic differential scales.

Rating data were obtained under these conditions, and the results are summarized as follows.

Roughly speaking, there was an overall average of approximately 90 seconds for the time that the listeners ran the tapes for themselves. One conclusion was that if a tape were two minutes in length it would give all listeners of this population sufficient time to judge the stimulus materials. A second finding was that the average amount of time taken to fill in the scales on the ethnicity-nonstandardness and the confidence-eagerness dimensions were not significantly different from one another. This generally nullified the concern of whether judgments on one dimension might confound (in time) judgments on another.

Stereotype measures. As was mentioned earlier, the Texas study included a measurement situation where teachers were presented with a label of a type of child, and were asked to fill out the semantic differential scales based upon their experience with such children. A third pilot study represented attempts to determine the feasibility of such measures. In summary, a variety of capsule descriptions were prepared of Anglo, Black, and Mexican-American children of middle and lower status. One example of these descriptions, that of a lower-class Mexican-American child is as follows:

He is a Mexican-American boy who comes from a family of 10. His father is a gas station attendant. He lives in a lower-class neighborhood.

These descriptions, as well as additional videotapes of children from the three ethnic groups and the two status levels were presented to groups of teachers and teacher candidates, and rating data were obtained. Such data were gathered in terms of first rating the written descriptions, then approximately two weeks later rating videotapes, and finally repeating ratings of the same capsule descriptions.

One major focus in the analyses was to determine if valid and reliable ratings could be obtained in response to the capsule descriptions. Generally, this was the case. Validity was assessed by the degree to which differentiations were made of the capsule descriptions of different types of children in approximately the same pattern that they were made of videotapes. Reliability was again assessed in terms of intraclass correlational methods. Results were positive on both accounts. One somewhat unexpected finding of this study was the extreme consistency of the ratings of the capsule descriptions across the two-week period. Ratings of all the capsules were almost precisely the same for the two rating periods. Of theoretical interest to us was the degree to which stereotype ratings were similar to the videotape ratings. At best, it can be said that there was a moderate correlation between ratings of the capsule descriptions and ratings of videotapes of children who would fall into categories intended by the capsuled description. This correlation was, as might be expected, not perfect, but there was enough correspondence to warrant further study of such a relationship in the main Texas field work. In subsequent, more formal work, it was found that teachers, just as they would rate capsule descriptions of children, would also rate labels of children of different ethnic groups, such as "Black," "Anglo," and the like. Labels rather than capsuled descriptions, were eventually used in the main phase of this research.

The Main Texas Study: Ethnicity, Experience, and Expectations[5]

Purpose

In overview, this research involved having in-service teachers evaluate videotapes taken to represent Anglo, Black, and Mexican-American children from the Central Texas area. Teachers were also asked to provide speech evaluations of children based upon their average experiences with Anglo, Black, and Mexican-American pupil groups. In one condition, teachers were given only a label instead of a videotape as a stimulus. These label ratings were intended to index teachers' speech stereotypes of children in the three ethnic groups. For both videotape and label ratings teachers were also asked to assign a child to a particular class level (1 = remedial, 2 = below average . . . 5 = well above average) in the following subjects: art, grammar, physical education, social studies, mathematics, spelling, music, composition, and reading. These assignments were taken as an index of teachers' expectations of pupils' performance in various subject matter areas. Given this body of rating data, specific questions of research were as follows:

1. What are the relations of teacher experience and ethnicity to the differentiation of videotape speech samples of Anglo, Black, and Mexican-American children?
2. What are the relations of teacher experience and ethnicity to the differentiation of stereotype labels of Anglo, Black, and Mexican-American children?
3. To what degree can speech ratings based upon stereotypes be used to predict ratings of videotaped samples?
4. To what degree can speech ratings based upon either videotaped samples or stereotype labels be used to predict teachers' expectations of pupils' academic performances?

---

[5]This study was reported in Williams, Frederick, Whitehead, J. L., and Miller, L. "Relations between Language Attitudes and Teacher Expectancy," *American Educational Research Journal,* 1972, *9,* 263-277. Copyright by the American Educational Research Association, Washington, D. C.

Method

Subjects. The teachers were from fifteen elementary schools in the Central Texas area. A promise of anonymity prevents the identification of the individual schools, but some 60% of the teachers were from towns under 35,000 in population, while the remainder were from larger areas. A total of 175 teachers participated in the evaluations which were included in the present analyses.[6] A desire for teacher stratification by ethnicity and experience level led to the division of this total number of teachers into five experience groups (0-4 years, 5-9, 10-19, 20-29, over 30) with 25 Anglo teachers and 10 Black teachers within each.

Materials. Language samples used in the field research were drawn from the collection of videotapes described in the previous section of this chapter. In a given testing session, a group of teachers saw six different videotapes, each approximately two minutes in duration. These six videotapes represented a randomized sequence of Anglo, Black, and Mexican-American children each from the two status levels. Four different test sequences, each involving different children but representing the same ethnic and status categories, were prepared for the field work. By systematically rotating the tapes for different test groups, data for the study represented a nearly equal frequency of administration of the four different tapes.

The semantic differential scales and the overall evaluation form appear in Figure 4.1. The lower part of the form contains the scales for assignments of a child to graded classes. Nine different academic subjects are listed. Each subject had the opportunity to assign a child to graded classes of 1-5 in each of these subjects.

Subjects' test booklets contained a first sheet for demographic data, a second sheet which explained the guise of the experiment,[7] and the third sheet which explained how to use the semantic differential scales. Following these instructional forms were three evaluation forms, each with an ethnic label in the upper right-hand corner. The remaining six pages of the booklet were numbered 1-6 to correspond with the six videotapes that were to be presented to the subjects.

Procedures. Teachers' evaluations were provided within the context of an in-service training program on the topic of "language differences in children." Instructions and the videotape evaluations comprised the first segment of this

---

[6] Eighteen Mexican-American teachers were also tested in the field work. However, this sample was too small for inclusion in the present analyses. Separate analyses are reported in Miller (1972) and later in this chapter.

[7] The guise was to see different children as a basis for an in-service training program.

FIGURE 4.1
NOTE: Items 3, 4, 5, 11, and 15 are filler scales.

EVALUATION FORM

1.   Please give ratings of the child on the following scales:
   (1) THE CHILD SEEMS: unsure   〇〇〇〇〇〇〇   confident
   (2) THE LANGUAGE OF THE CHILD'S HOME IS PROBABLY:
           standard American   〇〇〇〇〇〇〇   marked ethnic style
   (3) THE CHILD SEEMS: intelligent   〇〇〇〇〇〇〇   unintelligent
   (4) THE CHILD PROBABLY SPENDS:
           little   〇〇〇〇〇〇〇   much time away from home
   (5) THE CHILD SEEMS TO BE: sad   〇〇〇〇〇〇〇   happy
   (6) THE CHILD SOUNDS: Anglo-like   〇〇〇〇〇〇〇   non-Anglo like
   (7) THE CHILD'S HOME LIFE IS PROBABLY: like   〇〇〇〇〇〇〇   unlike yours
   (8) THE CHILD IS: active   〇〇〇〇〇〇〇   passive
   (9) THE CHILD SEEMS: reticent   〇〇〇〇〇〇〇   eager to speak
   (10) THE CHILD'S FAMILY IS PROBABLY: low   〇〇〇〇〇〇〇   high social status
   (11) THE CHILD IS: determined   〇〇〇〇〇〇〇   not determined in school
   (12) THE CHILD SEEMS: hesitant   〇〇〇〇〇〇〇   enthusiastic
   (13) THE CHILD SEEMS CULTURALLY: disadvantaged   〇〇〇〇〇〇〇   advantaged
   (14) THE CHILD SEEMS TO: like   〇〇〇〇〇〇〇   dislike talking
   (15) THE CHILD SEEMS: non-competitive   〇〇〇〇〇〇〇   competitive

2.   Now (using the code below), please assign the child
       to graded classes in the following subjects:

SUBJECT	Graded Class
ART	▌▐▐▐▐
GRAMMAR	▌▐▐▐▐
PHYS. ED.	▌▐▐▐▐
SOC. STUD.	▌▐▐▐▐
MATHEMATICS	▌▐▐▐▐
SPELLING	▌▐▐▐▐
MUSIC	▌▐▐▐▐
COMPOSITION	▌▐▐▐▐
READING	▌▐▐▐▐

GRADED CLASS CODE
1 = remedial class
2 = below average class
3 = average class
4 = above average class
5 = far above average class

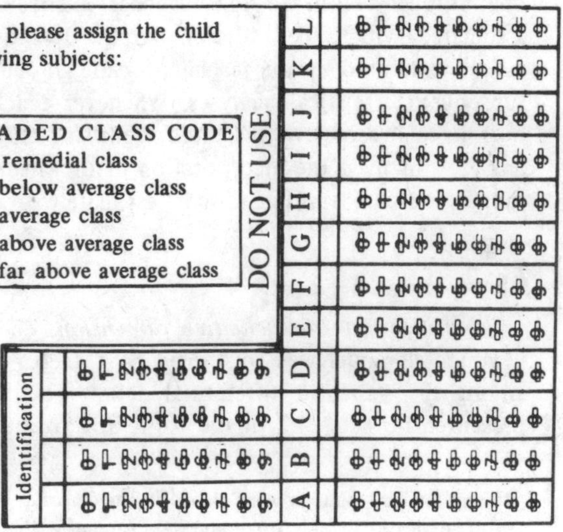

DO NOT USE

program. Testing was followed by the instructional materials for the in-service training, which drew in part from the videotapes which had been presented to the teachers. Evaluations were gathered in subgroups of teachers averaging approximately ten persons per session.

Data gathering took place in the schools, and most often in a space set aside in a library. Typically, two researchers conducted the evaluation session, having been introduced to the teachers as the staff for the in-service training session. The videotapes and the booklets were presented to the teachers as materials for the in-service training session along with the instructions which encouraged the teachers' frank opinions of these children in terms of the items on the evaluation sheet. After instruction in the use of the evaluation form, teacher-evaluators were told to begin marking the first three sheets of the evaluation booklet, each of which contained a label representing children of a particular ethnic group. The teachers were asked to provide evaluations of their average or anticipated experiences with children in each of these groups. It should be noted that teachers had the option of marking the neutral point on any of the evaluation scales and a "no decision" option on the placement in the various graded classes. Videotapes were played through an 11-inch monitor with sufficient time after each selection for evaluators to complete their response scales. Each teacher-evaluator responded to one of the four tape sequences which incorporated a child in each of the ethnic groups and each of the two status levels. The four stimulus tapes were systematically rotated such that each was used with equal frequency.

Teachers' responses to semantic differential scales were scored by assigning one through seven to the response entries where the one was arbitrarily associated with a cell adjacent to the less desirable adjective. The numeric assignments used by the teachers for the graded classes were used directly in the subsequent statistical analyses. Whenever teachers marked the "no decision" option, their scores were treated as missing data, which in subsequent statistical analyses involved the incorporation of the mean of the distribution of scores on that scale as the least biased score estimate.

Results

Identification of evaluative dimensions. The existence of the two-factor judgmental model was confirmed by a factor analysis of the intercorrelations among the semantic differential data.[8] The results of the final analysis are presented in Table 4.2 in the form of a rotated matrix of the factor structure

---

[8]In this analysis, unities were placed in the diagonal of the correlation matrix, and factors with latent roots greater than one were rotated with Varimax criteria.

TABLE 4.2

Rotated Factor Matrix of Teacher Responses to 10
Semantic Differential Scales

	Factors	
Variables	I	II
1. unsure	.73	.27
2. marked ethnic style	.12	.83
3. non-Anglo-like	.12	.81
4. home life unlike yours	.24	.79
5. passive	.72	.16
6. reticent	.85	.18
7. low social status	.50	.63
8. hesitant	.81	.22
9. disadvantaged	.51	.63
10. dislike talking	.71	.14
Percentage of total variance	(35.3%)	(29.7%)

and where filler scales are omitted. As in the Chicago study (Williams, 1970b) and in the pilot work, the two-factor model had dimensions interpretable as *confidence-eagerness* and *ethnicity-nonstandardness*. Given evidence of the judgmental model, the ten scale scores were reduced to two-factor scores by summing over the five scales that had been identified with each of the two factors. Accordingly, factor scores for confidence-eagerness could range from five to thirty-five, where the higher score, the greater the rated confidence-eagerness of the child. Scores on ethnicity-nonstandardness represented the same range; however, a high score would represent a lesser amount of ethnicity-nonstandardness associated with the stimulus.

Rating differences. An assumption of the study was that children from low-status families would typically be rated as less confident and eager and more ethnic-nonstandard than children from middle-status families, and that Anglo children would be rated differently on these two variables as compared with children from the Black and Mexican-American speech communities. A test of this assumption, as well as the research question of effects of teacher ethnicity and experience level, was undertaken in the form of two identical four-way analyses of variance, one each for the confidence-eagerness and the ethnicity-nonstandardness factor scores. A summary table of the two analyses is presented in Table 4.3.

TABLE 4.3
Analyses of Variance of Confidence-Eagerness and Ethnicity-Nonstandardness Ratings

Source	d.f.	Confidence-Eagerness		Ethnicity-Nonstandardness	
		MS	F	MS	F
Between Subjects					
A (experience)	4	57.0	1.1	57.9	1.1
B (teach. ethnicity)	1	141.1	2.6	322.1	6.4**
AB	4	48.5	.9	25.1	.5
error	165	54.2		50.6	
Within Subjects					
C (child status)	1	5751.3	83.5**	1745.4	35.6**
AC	4	161.0	2.3	63.1	1.3
BC	1	32.2	.5	2.7	.1
ABC	4	46.1	.7	139.4	2.8*
error	165	68.8		49.0	
D (child ethnicity)	2	554.7	11.1**	6571.8	86.2**
AD	8	41.4	.8	46.7	.6
BD	2	17.1	.3	422.1	5.5**
ABD	8	20.7	.4	37.4	.5
error	330	50.1		76.2	
CD	2	928.6	27.7**	186.7	7.3**
ACD	8	25.7	.8	15.9	.6
BCD	2	96.8	2.9	59.6	2.3
ABCD	8	32.9	1.0	27.3	1.1
error	330	33.6		25.7	

**$p < .01$ *$p < .05$

Analysis of confidence-eagerness ratings revealed that there were no significant differences among means due to teachers' levels of experience (0-4 years = 23.0; ·5-9 = 23.3; 10-19 = 22.3; 20-29 = 22.8; >· 30 = 22.2), teacher ethnicity (Black = 23.0, Anglo = 22.5) nor any interactions between these variables. Neither did these variables interact with any of the child characteristics. In short, confidence-eagerness ratings appeared independent of the teacher characteristics included in this study.

TABLE 4.4

Means of Confidence-Eagerness Ratings in the Child
Status by Ethnicity Interaction

Ethnicity:		Anglo	Black	Mexican-American
Status:	Low	23.0_c*	18.3_a	20.2_b
	Middle	26.1_d	27.6_e	23.3_c

*Means with common subscripts are not significantly ($p < .05$) different from one another (Duncan Multiple Range Test).

As assumed earlier, there were differences in ratings according to child status and ethnicity. The interpretation of these was found within the significant interaction between these two variables, the means of which are compared in Table 4.4. Children from the low-status groups were, on the average, rated lower in confidence-eagerness than children from the middle-status families. In the low-status groups, as expected, Anglo children were generally rated higher in confidence-eagerness than the children from the minority groups. However, this assumption was not sustained in the middle-status groups. Here there was a reversal with the Black children rated as slightly more confident and eager than the Anglo children, but both were rated as significantly higher than Mexican-American children.

There were no significant differences in ethnicity-nonstandardness ratings according to teacher experience (Table 4.3). There was a significant three-way interaction which involved the teacher ethnicity variable with the variables of teacher experience and child status. As Table 4.5 shows, an examination of the pattern of the 20 means involved in this interaction revealed that low-status children were generally rated as more ethnic and nonstandard than middle-status ones. However, the magnitude of these differences varied in an uninterpretable pattern according to particular combinations of teacher experience and ethnicity.

Additionally, there was a significant (Table 4.3) difference in ratings of ethnicity-nonstandardness according to the ethnicity of the teacher (Black = 20.1; Anglo = 18.6). Significant differences also were found in the interaction of teacher ethnicity and child ethnicity. As shown in Table 4.6, the general pattern was that although Black and Anglo teachers tended to rate Anglo children as less ethnic and nonstandard as compared to minority group children, Black teachers rated the minority group children as less ethnic and nonstandard as compared

TABLE 4.5

*Mean of Ethnicity-Nonstandardness Ratings in the
Interaction of Teacher Experience, Teacher
Ethnicity, and Child Status*

Teachers: Anglo, Black   Stimuli: Videotape

Child status:	Low		Middle	
Teacher Ethnicity:	Anglo	Black	Anglo	Black
Teacher Experience:				
0-4 yrs.	16.3_a*	18.5_{abc}	20.1_{cdefgh}	22.0_{fgh}
5-9	20.0_{cdefg}	18.4_{abc}	19.1_{bcde}	21.6_{efgh}
10-19	16.8_{ab}	19.7_{cdef}	21.1_{cdefgh}	19.4_{bcdef}
20-29	18.8_{abcd}	18.3_{abc}	21.1_{cdefgh}	23.7_h
30	17.0_{ab}	19.9_{cdefg}	21.3_{defgh}	22.5_{gh}

*Means with common subscripts are not significantly $(p < .05)$ different from one another.

TABLE 4.6

*Means of Ethnicity-Nonstandardness Ratings in the
Teacher Ethnicity by Child Ethnicity Interaction*

Teacher Ethnicity:		Anglo	Black
Child Ethnicity:	Anglo	25.8_c*	24.5_c
	Black	14.2_a	17.7_b
	Mexican-American	17.5_b	19.0_b

*Means with common subscripts are not significantly $(p < .05)$ different from one another (Duncan Multiple Range Test).

with the Anglo teachers' ratings. In short, either Anglo teachers perceived Black and Mexican-American children as more ethnic-nonstandard, or Black teachers perceived them as less so, or both.

TABLE 4.7
Means of Ethnicity-Nonstandardness Ratings in the Child Status by Ethnicty Interaction

Ethnicity:		Anglo	Black	Mexican-American
Income Level:	Low	23.7_d*	13.7_a	17.7_b
	Middle	26.6_e	18.2_{bc}	18.9_c

*Means with common subscripts are not significantly ($p < .05$) different from one another (Duncan Multiple Range Test).

As in the case of the confidence-eagerness ratings, the assumption of status differences among the children was confirmed. The means of a significant child status by ethnicity interaction are given in Table 4.7. Here it is shown that low-status children were rated, on the average, as more ethnic-nonstandard than the children from middle-status families. Also, Anglo children were rated as less ethnic-nonstandard, as compared with the Black and Mexican-American children.

Stereotyping. As described earlier, it was assumed that teachers' ratings of their average and expected experiences with children as labeled for the three ethnic groups would provide data approximating the stereotypes of these children in terms of the two-factor model. An assessment of the relation between these stereotyped ratings and the ratings of the videotaped presentations was undertaken by the çalculation of a regression of the latter scores upon the former. Separate equations were calculated for the variables of confidence-eagerness and ethnicity-nonstandardness. Further, separate equations were calculated for both of these within the two child status groups.

Results of the regression equations (Table 4.8) were interpreted as follows: (1) A statistically significant but negligible magnitude of correlation was found between stereotyped ratings on confidence-eagerness and the ratings of videotapes of low-status children. (2) No correlation on confidence-eagerness was observed between stereotypes and videotapes for the children from middle-income families. (3) By contrast, stereotyped ratings of ethnicity-nonstandardness showed moderate correlations with videotaped ratings for both low- and middle-status groups of children.

The general answer to questions of stereotyping was that there is a moderate degree of relation between stereotyped ratings of ethnicity-nonstandardness and videotaped ratings of the children.

TABLE 4.8

Prediction of Videotape Ratings from
Stereotype Ratings

Rating/Subgroup	Coefficients			
	a	b	R	R^2
Confidence-Eagerness				
(low status)	15.8	.200	.19*	.037
(middle status)	22.9	.042	.04	.002
Ethnicity-Nonstandardness				
(low status)	9.2	.500	.48*	.232
(middle status)	12.1	.389	.40*	.157

*$*p < .01$ with d.f. = 503

Teacher expectancy. Based upon intercorrelations among the class assignments to the subject matter areas, it was possible to reduce the nine subject variables to three. These were: *Language arts* (average assignments in grammar, spelling, composition and reading); *Language arts-related* (mathematics, social studies); and *Non-language arts* (music, arts, physical education). As implied by these labels, it was assumed that intercorrelations among the individual assignments were evidence of a general differentiation of subject matter according to the degree of involvement of language arts materials. These averaged scores were subsequently employed in three two-variable regression equations, each one corresponding to a regression of class-level assignments in a subject area upon the videotape ratings of confidence-eagerness and ethnicity-nonstandardness. Results (Table 4.9) of the three equations were interpreted in terms of multiple correlation coefficients, determination coefficients, and the relative proportions of variance predicted by confidence-eagerness and ethnicity-nonstandardness ratings.

Although graded class assignments in all three areas could be predicted upon the basis of the language evaluations, two patterns were evident in these results. One apparent generalization was that, as might be expected, the more the subject matter areas are directly related to language arts the better the evaluation of the child's language serves as a predictor of teacher expectancy. A second generalization was that the more a subject area involves language arts, the more ratings of ethnicity-nonstandardness rather than confidence-eagerness will serve as a dominant predictor of teacher expectancy.

TABLE 4.9

Predictions of Class-Level Assignments
from Confidence-Eagerness and
Ethnicity-Nonstandardness Ratings

Stimulus Class	R	R^2	Relative Contributions	
			Confidence-Eagerness	Ethnicity-Nonstandardness
Videotapes				
Language Arts	.70*	.488	.17	.32
Math-Soc. St.	.61*	.377	.16	.21
Music-Art-P.E.	.36*	.129	.12	.01

*$p < .01$ for d.f. = 1156

Discussion

Summary. Generalizations of the results were as follows:

1. As found in past studies, teachers tended to give global evaluations of language samples along dimensions identified as confidence-eagerness and ethnicity-nonstandardness.

2. Teachers' amount of experience appears unrelated in any interpretable way to ratings of confidence-eagerness or ethnicity-nonstandardness.

3. Teacher ethnicity and child ethnicity interact in terms of minority group children being rated generally less ethnic-nonstandard by Black teachers than by Anglo teachers.

4. Only in evaluations of ethnicity-nonstandardness do teachers' stereotype ratings of children appear to be related to ratings of videotape language samples.

5. Teachers' expectations of children's performance in subject matters are partially predictable upon the basis of language attitudes; the degree of prediction increases when the subject matter area is directly within the language arts.

Implications. The close association between teachers' language attitudes and expectations in language arts subjects can be viewed within several of the issues which have emerged from contemporary urban language studies (Labov 1966; Shuy, *et al.* 1967). The main linguistic variable in these studies has been dialect, which is presumed to be a function of the grammatical system that a child is using. Another variable is fluency, which is performance variation related to the formality of the speech situation. It seems worth speculating that the two dimensions of evaluation found in the present and earlier studies are attitudinal correlates of two of the main variables found in urban language studies. That is, ratings of confidence-eagerness seem to reflect perception of fluency in a situation. Ratings of ethnicity-nonstandardness may be a direct reflection of the grammatical characteristics exhibited in the child's language.

This correspondence between language characteristics and language attitudes prompts considerations of a major problem discussed in many contemporary urban language studies. This is the tendency of teachers and educational researchers to confuse language differences with deficits. As argued by the urban language researchers, most minority group children are developing quite normal and adequate linguistic systems to meet the demands of their individual speech communities. Although it may be accurate for a teacher to evaluate a child's language as ethnic and nonstandard or reticent, it may be quite inaccurate to always expect this performance in all speech situations.

The moderate relation between stereotyped ratings of ethnicity-nonstandardness and ratings of the videotapes suggests that teachers to some degree may be fulfilling their own expectations even in the evaluations of children. This predisposition, too, requires further exploration. To what degree in evaluating the speech of the child do teachers differ in their capability of being sensitive to dialect variations relative to their stereotyped attitudes? Evidence in the present research shows a greater variability among Black teachers' ratings than among those of Anglo teachers. Perhaps this is a function of the Black teachers' more direct experience with both standard and Black dialects of English.

One of the most practical implications of this research is that given the relationship between language attitudes and teacher expectancy, there is a suggestion that the study of language variations in children, particularly minority group children, and attitudinal correlates be introduced into the curricula of teacher training. To prevent language attitudes from serving as false prophecies, or worse yet becoming themselves self-fulfilled prophecies, teachers should be trained to be sensitive to variations in social dialects and variations in performance. Language evaluation, which incorporates the attitudinal side of the social dialect coin, could be included as part of the teacher training process. The present project not only points to the need for such training but provides a number of ideas for implementation and evaluation of the results of training.

Evaluation Results of Mexican-American
and Anglo Teachers

Problem

This research was an analysis of data from the main Texas project, but with a focus on Mexican-American teachers (who were insufficiently represented to be included in the analyses just discussed). This study (portions reprinted from Miller, 1972) sought answers to the following questions:

(1) Are there differences in the stereotypes of Mexican-American and Anglo teachers with regard to Mexican-American and Anglo children's speech and academic performance?
(2) Are there differences in the videotape ratings of children with regard to child status?
(3) Are there differences in videotape ratings of children with regard to child ethnicity?

Data

Teachers in this study were 18 Mexican-American and 18 Anglo staff members from the same schools in Central Texas. The Anglos were selected from the larger number described in the previous section upon the basis of similar experience levels and the same schools as the Mexican-Americans. Rating data from these teachers were of the same type as already described, except that evaluations of Black children were omitted.

Analyses and Results

Stereotype ratings. To answer the first question—whether differences in teacher ethnicity resulted in differences in stereotype judgments of speech characteristics and graded class assignments—five two-way analyses of variance were calculated, one for each dependent variable. Independent variables were teacher ethnicity and child ethnicity.

Results indicated that only language arts-related ratings (*social studies, mathematics*) showed a statistically significant difference due to teacher ethnicity. Comparison of the means revealed that Anglo teachers rated all children lower (2.7) in related language arts classes than did Mexican-American teachers (3.0). This difference had generality across ratings of both Anglo and Mexican-American children.

On all class expectancy ratings except the non-language arts (*music, art, physical education*), there was a significant difference due to child ethnicity. The

TABLE 4.10

Mean Ratings for Child Ethnicity

Dependent Variable	Child Ethnicity	
	Anglo	Mexican-American
confidence-eagerness	25.5_a*	20.3_b
ethnicity-nonstandardness	9.4_a	21.7_b
language arts	3.2_a	2.9_b
related language arts	3.3_a	2.4_b
unrelated language arts	3.1_a	3.3_a

*Different alphabetical subscripts indicate significant ($p < .05$) differences.

pertinent means are summarized in Table 4.10. In general, Anglo children were stereotyped as more confident, less ethnic-sounding, and better in language arts and related language arts subjects. Anglo and Mexican-American children were not rated significantly different in subjects unrelated to language arts.

Videotape ratings. In order to answer the questions regarding differences in child status and child ethnicity, five three-way analyses of variance were calculated with teacher ethnicity, child status, and child ethnicity as independent variables and language judgments and academic expectancies as dependent variables.

Child status and child ethnicity had a significant interaction for the variables of confidence-eagerness, language arts, related language arts, and unrelated language arts. None of these four interactions indicated differences between status groups for Anglo children, but all distinguished between Mexican-American children. The middle-status Mexican-American was rated as more confident and a better student in all the academic areas than the low-status Mexican-American child. The means are summarized in Table 4.11. In other words, the status variable was ineffective for Anglo children but differentiated the Mexican-American children.

In addition to the interaction between child ethnicity and child status described above, teacher ethnicity interacted with child ethnicity for the variable of unrelated language arts. The means are summarized in Table 4.12. Again, Anglo children were not judged significantly different on art, music, and physical education by either Anglo or Mexican-American teachers. However,

TABLE 4.11
Means Described in the Interactions

CONFIDENCE-EAGERNESS

		Anglo	Mexican-American
Status	Low	24.5_b*	17.0_c
	Middle	24.6_b	27.3_a

LANGUAGE ARTS

		Anglo	Mexican-American
Status	Low	3.2_b	2.8_c
	Middle	3.2_b	3.6_a

RELATED LANGUAGE ARTS

		Anglo	Mexican-American
Status	Low	3.0_b	2.6_c
	Middle	3.2_{ab}	3.4_a

UNRELATED LANGUAGE ARTS

		Anglo	Mexican-American
Status	Low	3.3_{ab}	3.1_b
	Middle	3.1_b	3.4_a

*Different alphabetical subscripts indicate significant ($p < .05$) differences.

TABLE 4.12
Means for Unrelated Language Arts:
Teacher Ethnicity with Child Ethnicity

Teacher	Child	
	Anglo	Mexican-American
Mexican-American	3.2_b*	3.5_a
Anglo	3.2_b	3.0_b

*Different alphabetical subscripts indicate significant ($p < .05$) differences.

Mexican-American children were rated most favorably by Mexican-American teachers (3.5) and least favorably (3.0) by Anglo teachers on these subjects.

Finally, on the variable of ethnicity-nonstandardness teachers significantly differentiated children on the basis of status. Low-status children across both ethnicities were judged as more ethnic-sounding (17.0) than middle-status children (9.1). No significant differences were realized with regard to child ethnicity.

Discussion

Several generalizations seem to emerge from the above results. First, with regard to stereotypes, it is interesting to note the similarity of the results with those of Lambert's French and English Canadian study. In this instance both Anglo and Mexican-American teachers held similar stereotypes of their school population as indicated by the fact that Anglo children were thought to possess more confidence and be less ethnic-sounding as well as have higher academic expectancies than their Mexican-American counterparts. This community-wide stereotype phenomenon suggests that both Anglo and Mexican-American teachers tended to view their students in a similar light. This similarity of view is also reflected in videotape ratings of children. Here, again, teacher ethnicity did not reveal any significant differences in rating behavior. Thus, a student in this study has no basis for believing that because his teacher is of the same or different ethnicity she will have different expectancies or preconceived stereotypes of him.

Second, with regard to the ratings elicited by children on videotape, it appears that the social status of the Mexican-American child will be a more important factor in making language and academic judgments than the status of the Anglo child. Low-class and middle-class Anglos were not rated as significantly different on four out of the five variables, but the low- and middle-class Mexican-American children were differentiated on this variable with the middle-class child rated consistently more favorably. The one variable on which teachers of different ethnicities varied was that of unrelated language arts assignments (music, arts, physical education). In this instance, Mexican-American teachers rated Mexican-American children as having better capabilities and Anglo teachers rated Anglo children as having better capabilities.

In summary, one can only speculate as to why teachers of different ethnicities hold similar stereotypes and make similar judgments of children's speech and academic performance. One reason, which is of course only speculation, is that teachers of a minority race may have internalized the values and expectations of the majority either through educational pressures or personal choice. Thus, in some respects the student may be misled if he feels that a teacher of his own ethnicity may have a different or more accurate insight into his capabilities and cultural differences.

Whereas the main body of the Texas research has concentrated on how the teachers differentiated the children and how these differentiations were related to academic attitudes, the next study by Williams and Naremore[9] focused upon the ways teachers can be differentiated by their linguistic attitudes.

A Follow-Up Study of Teacher Differences

One major restriction on the generality of the interpretations of the main Texas study was that, except for ethnicity and amount of experience, teacher differences have not been thoroughly investigated. The study by Naremore reported in Chapter 3 used a variation of factor analytic techniques (Q-analysis; Stephenson, 1953) to group teachers into four categories based upon commonality of their rating behaviors. Results showed some division of teachers by race—one group was all Anglos—but mostly divisions in terms of some teachers rating all Black children consistently low or high on selected scales, somewhat independent of the children's actual performance. However, the results of her study were somewhat restricted because of the small number of teachers involved and because about a third of the teachers were factorally complex (i.e., their ratings identified them with several groups rather than with one group type).

The present study was a similar type Q-analysis, but one which involved Black, Anglo, and Mexican-American teachers from the studies conducted in Central Texas (Williams, et al., 1971a). In order to come within the limits of the Q-analysis computer program used in the present research, 130 teachers were selected at random from a total of 193 originally involved in the field study. The ethnic subgroups in the present analyses were 85 Anglos, 13 Mexican-Americans and 32 Blacks.

The data included three major components: (1) ratings by the teachers of videotaped speech samples of Black, Mexican-American, and Anglo children; (2) ratings of speech expected from these ethnic groups of children (a stereotype rating obtained by a response to a label), and (3) ratings of the academic expectancy in language arts subjects of children from these three groups. The Q-analysis was conducted to determine if ratings of the videotapes would indicate heterogeneity among the teachers' rating behaviors. Given evidence of different teacher rating types, teacher characteristics could be contrasted in terms of ethnicity, rating biases, and school characteristics. Generalizations about these teacher rating biases could then be evaluated by comparing them

---

[9]Subsequently published. See Williams and Naremore, 1974.

with mean language stereotype and academic expectancy ratings in language arts provided by each teacher type.

Q-Analysis

The factor analysis was accomplished by use of an extended factoring program, QUANAL, using the form of inverted matrix analysis related to Stephenson's Q-analysis. In this analysis, the scores given on each scale were standardized by rows and by columns, thus assuring comparable distributions of scores across both respondents and scales. The correlation matrix was evaluated for principal component factors based upon the criterion that any factor (to be called *teacher type*) must consist of at least four teachers loading above .40. Varimax rotation was performed in the traditional manner. A second phase of the analysis provided a summary of the results in terms of how the use of the rating scales across types of children distinguished the teacher types.[10] Through the use of summary and comparative tables provided from this analysis, it was possible to discover what kinds of judgmental behavior occurred for any teacher type and exactly where and how any two teacher types differed in their ratings of the type of children on the different scales. It is important to remember that the discussion of the teachers' judgmental behavior is based on the weighted summary scores for teacher types rather than on the scores of any individual teachers in the groups.

Results and Discussion

The factor structure. Based on the criteria discussed above, five factors were extracted in the analysis, together accounting for 59% of the total variance. In essence, each of these factors represented types of teachers who had some pattern or patterns in common in the way they rated particular kinds of children on particular scales. For purposes of interpretation, it should be noted that no factor or group of teachers is "pure" in the sense that the teachers were precisely alike in their rating behavior. The assignment of teachers to factors is done in a relative sense, based upon individual teachers' rating behaviors being more like the behavior of teachers in one given group than in another. Space limitations prevent the reproduction of the rotated factor matrix here, but a number of its characteristics are summarized in Table 4.13. In general, about one-half of the teachers were grouped into one dominant factor (*Teacher type*), about one-fourth into a second factor, and the remaining one-fourth distributed among

---

[10]These distinctions were determined by a process in which the individual teachers on a given factor were assigned weights relative to their degree of loading on the factor. These weights were used in computing a listing of z-scores assigned to the different observations by the group as a whole.

TABLE 4.13
Factor Characteristics

Factor (Teacher Type)	N*	Variance %	Average loading
I	62	27%	.74
II	30	13	.69
III	14	7	.66
IV	8	7	.70
V	8	5	.51

*Eight teachers who were factorally complex and/or loaded negatively are omitted from this summary.

three minor factors. Average loadings of teachers on the factors within which they were typed is roughly at the same level for four of the factors. This average is sufficiently high to suggest that most teachers loaded predominantly on single factors as against partial loadings on multiple factors. Only in Factor V is there an indication that the teacher type may be less homogeneous and concentrated on that factor.

Teacher characteristics. Table 4.14 summarizes various information gathered about the teachers and their schools. Some major contrasts among the different teacher types were as follows: Type I, II, and III teachers are predominantly Anglo as against IV and V being Black or Mexican-American. The relative percentage of males is greater for Type IV than for the others. Types IV and V have an average of several years more teaching experience than the other types. Type II teachers work in schools of predominantly Anglo students, whereas Types III and IV have relatively large proportions of Mexican-American students, and Types I and V racially balanced groups. More than other characteristics, ethnicity of teacher and student population—as in the earlier research—appeared to stand out here.

One potential bias not shown in Table 4.14 was that 77% of the Type II teachers had responded to only one of the four different stimulus tapes, whereas other teacher types had responded to a mixture of stimulus tapes. This meant that one reason for the definition of Type II teachers was that their similarities in rating a certain set of tapes may have caused them to fall on one factor.

Ratings distinguishing teacher types. As discussed earlier, the analyses provided a summary of scales and stimuli to which teachers of a given type responded alike, and those responses which separated them from other groups. A

TABLE 4.14

Teacher Characteristics

Characteristics	Teacher ethnicity			Sex		Average years teaching	Highest degree		
	Anglo	Black	Mex.-Am.	f.	m.		BA	BA	BA
Type I	71%	24%	5%	87%	13%	7.2 yrs.	5%	74%	21%
II	70	20	10	72	28	5.5	0	67	33
III	79	21	0	57	43	7.4	7	64	29
IV	0	38	62	38	62	9.6	13	50	37
V	25	50	25	62	38	9.8	12	63	25

TABLE 4.14 (continued)

Characteristics	School type			Predominant ethnicity of students			
	Urban	Rural	Comb.	Anglo	Black	Mex.-Am.	Mixed
Type I	53%	19%	28%	31%	31%	20%	18%
II	46	7	47	66	3	24	7
III	71	22	7	21	14	50	15
IV	50	38	12	25	0	63	12
V	67	17	16	25	25	25	25

summary of these rating similarities, given in Table 4.15, lends insight into the rating biases of each type. Subsequently it was possible to compare these rating biases with average stereotype ratings for each teacher type, in order to determine whether the teacher types' reactions to the videotapes were related to their stereotype reactions.

In broad interpretation, Type I teachers, about half the raters involved in the entire study, had a bias of rating Anglo children as both particularly confident and standard. The other four teacher types contrast with Type I mainly in bias toward particular minority groups on given rating factors. This might be expected as it may be recalled that in terms of teacher characteristics, except for the bias of the stimulus tape for Type II teachers, the types were mainly distinguished in terms of teacher and pupil ethnicity characteristics.

TABLE 4.15

*Summary of Videotape Ratings Which
Distinguished Each Teacher Type*

Type I: Rated middle-class Anglo children as particularly confident-eager
            and as not sounding ethnic and nonstandard.

Type II: Tended to rate middle-class Black and Mexican-American chil-
            dren as high on the confidence-eagerness scales, and low-class
            Black children as particularly ethnic and nonstandard. Some ev-
            idence of rating middle-class Anglo children lower than other
            teacher types on confidence-eagerness scales.

Type III: Rated middle-class Mexican-American children as particularly
            ethnic and nonstandard. Tended to rate lower-class Black chil-
            dren as relatively higher in confidence-eagerness than did other
            teacher types.

Type IV: Rated middle-class Black children as less ethnic and nonstandard
            and high in confidence-eagerness. Tended to rate lower-class
            Anglo children as low on confidence-eagerness.

Type V: Tended to rate low-class Black children as particularly low on
            confidence-eagerness.

It may be recalled that each teacher filled out the rating instrument in
response to labels representing the three ethnic groups of children. When these
measures are considered as stereotype ratings, they provide a basis for checking
on the generality of rating biases which most distinguished the different teacher
types. Thus it should be expected that if a teacher type tended to mark a child
on a videotape as high or low on a given factor and if this is an inherent bias of
the teachers that populated a rating type, then a similar bias should be revealed
in the stereotype ratings. Table 4.16 is a summary of the average stereotype
ratings for the five groups of teachers on each of the two factors for the three
types of children. Scores in this table represent the averaged sums of the five
scales (range = 5-35) for each of the two factors.

Based upon the rating biases found for Type I teachers, it is expected that
Anglo children should be rated numerically high by this group in terms of both
confidence-eagerness and ethnicity-nonstandardness (sounding standard). As
shown in Table 4.16, stereotype ratings reflected this bias. The ratings of Anglo
children on both confidence-eagerness and ethnicity-nonstandardness were

TABLE 4.16
Mean Stereotype Ratings

Factors:*	Confidence-Eagerness			Ethnicity-Nonstandardness		
Child Ethnicity:	Anglo	Black	Mex.-Am.	Anglo	Black	Mex.-Am.
Type I	26.8	22.1	18.1	26.6	12.5	13.0
II	26.7	22.3	17.2	26.5	14.2	13.1
III	25.5	22.9	19.8	23.9	17.4	10.4
IV	24.3	20.6	19.5	24.4	19.9	15.5
V	21.1	18.1	18.1	24.0	16.8	14.4

*The higher the value the more confident-eager and the *less* ethnic-nonstandard is the rating.

among the higher averages given by the groups.[11] This supports the generalization that Type I teachers tend to see Anglo children as sounding particularly confident and eager and as not particularly ethnic or nonstandard.

As noted in Table 4.15, Type II teachers had rated middle-class Black children as high in confidence-eagerness, and as shown in Table 4.16, their average ratings of the Black stereotype were among the highest of the five teacher types. By the same token, they tended to rate low-status Black children as particularly ethnic and nonstandard (low scores), and this bias appears in Table 4.16 in terms of stereotype ratings (although Type I teachers rated Black children as even more ethnic and nonstandard). Type II teachers had also tended to rate middle-class Mexican-American children as relatively high on confidence-eagerness. However, their average ratings in Table 4.16 indicate that they tended to rate their stereotype of Mexican-American children lower on confidence-eagerness. Thus their stereotype is a contradiction of the rating biases found in the earlier analysis of Mexican-American children. Finally, Type II teachers had tended to rate middle-class Anglo children as low on confidence-eagerness.

---

[11] Because of the ad hoc and basically descriptive nature of these comparisons, no statistical tests of rating differences were employed. There is also the problem of markedly different numbers of teachers on each factor.

However, there is another contradiction; as Table 4.16 indicates, there is no evidence of this in their average rating of the Anglo stereotype. In all, the overall congruence between the rating biases identified with Type II teachers and the stereotype biases is only partly evident. (As subsequently discussed, this may have been due to the biases of the stimulus tape which teachers of this type were concentrated on.)

Type III teachers, as noted earlier, had rated Mexican-American children as particularly ethnic- and nonstandard-sounding (low scores). As noted in Table 4.16, by far the lowest mean rating of Mexican-American children on ethnicity-nonstandardness is that of Type III teachers. These teachers had also tended to rate lower-class Black children as relatively high on confidence-eagerness. The results in Table 4.16 tended to corroborate this bias in that Type III ratings of Black children are the highest of all teachers on confidence-eagerness.

Type IV teacher ratings had indicated a bias in evaluating middle-class Black children as relatively less ethnic-nonstandard (high scores) as compared to other teacher groups. This bias is paralleled in Table 4.16 in that Type IV averages for Black children on ethnicity-nonstandardness are the highest of any teacher type. Also Type IV teachers had rated lower-class Anglo children as low on confidence-eagerness. There is slight evidence of a parallel for this in Table 4.16 in that the Type IV average for Anglo children is less on confidence-eagerness than for Types I, II and III but still higher than for Type V.

The main rating which distinguished Type V teachers was that they tended to rate lower-class Black children as low on confidence-eagerness. This is corroborated in Table 4.16; the Type V average for Black stereotypes are the lowest on confidence-eagerness for any teacher type.

As discussed earlier, prior research had indicated that teachers' academic expectancies for children were most predictable on the basis of relations between the language attitude ratings and expectancy in language arts subjects. Accordingly, the final analysis focused upon a contrast among the five types of teachers in terms of their stereotyped expectancies of the three ethnic groups in language arts subjects. The results are summarized in Table 4.17.

As discussed above, Type I teachers had a main bias of rating Anglo children high on both language attitude factors. This bias is somewhat corroborated in the expectancy results, in that Type I's highest expectancies in language arts subjects were for Anglo children, and this expectancy was generally higher than that found for any of the other four teacher groups.

The biases of Type II teachers, it may be recalled, were not always paralleled in the stereotype data. However, Type II teachers had tended to rate Black children as particularly ethnic and nonstandard. Accordingly their expectancies

TABLE 4.17
Expectancy in Language Arts*

Child Ethnicity:	Anglo	Black	Mex.-Am.
Type I	3.8	2.2	2.3
II	3.5	2.3	2.6
III	3.5	2.7	2.1
IV	2.9	2.8	2.3
V	2.7	2.4	2.3

*Rated on a 1-5 scale, 1 = "remedial," 5 = "far above average class."

of Black children should be relatively low in the language arts subjects, and the average rating as shown in Table 4.17 is evidence of this. No other marked parallels between language ratings and expectancy were evident for these teachers.

Rating biases in the videotape and stereotype data were generally compatible for Type III teachers in that Mexican-American children were rated as markedly ethnic and nonstandard, while Blacks were rated as high in confidence-eagerness. There are some parallels for these in the academic expectancy results. Type III's expectancy of Mexican-Americans in language arts subjects was the lowest not only for all pupil ethnic groups, but all teacher rating groups. By contrast, their expectancies for Black children were among the two highest found, although these are still substantially lower than some of those for Anglo children.

The main bias of Type IV teachers was in rating Black children as particularly nonethnic- and standard-sounding as compared with the other groups. There is slight evidence of this bias in their language arts expectancy data, in that they had the highest expectancies (but by only a small margin) for the Black stereotypes as compared with the other group's teachers.

Type V teachers' main distinguishing characteristic was that they tended to rate Black children low on confidence-eagerness. Although the distinction is relatively minimal, Type V's expectancy for Black children in language arts was among the lowest of the groups. (However, it could be noted that their expectations for all children were similarly low.)

Implications. The teacher rating types found in the study tend to be distinguished most in terms of attitude toward particular ethnic groups of children, with their ratings interacting with the teachers' own ethnicity and the predominant student ethnicities at their schools.

Except for Type II teachers, there was a general corroboration among rating biases, stereotype biases, and academic expectancies, all of which contributes to the interpretations regarding language attitudes and the heterogeneity of the teacher population. Type II teachers were very similar to Type I, except that they tended to vary slightly in terms of their ratings of minority group children and their schools had more Anglo students. The problem in interpreting these results is that most Type II teachers were also defined by common rating behavior biased toward the same videotape stimuli. At best, it might be generalized that Type II teachers are much like the Type I group—Anglo, Anglo attitudes—but that they are a particularly homogeneous subgroup of Type I in that they agreed so highly. on a particular stimulus tape. Their distinctions in rating behaviors, the bases for their factor definition, are as much a function of particular qualities of their homogeneity in regard to one stimulus tape as they are inherent biases observable in their stereotypes or academic expectancies.

Because the teachers for the Central Texas study did not constitute a random sample of a teacher population, it is not possible to say outright that the five subgroups of teachers represent a basis for segmenting teachers in the larger population. However it does seem safe to suggest that in a general way the attitude differences found in the present study could reflect types of contrasts in a larger population of teachers. It seems also quite reasonable to suggest that when there are variations in these attitudes, they will be highly tied to teacher ethnicity, possibly to the distribution of student ethnicities in the teachers' schools, and, of course, to stereotype biases which may be found in rating behaviors.

One important implication of these findings is that they raise a question about the assumption that teachers are a relatively homogeneous lot. Most of the design of curricula, educational programs, and entire school systems, reflects a general assumption that teachers, like classrooms, textbooks, and curriculum design, are standard components of the educational system which if integrated into the usual administrative formula will result in particular types of educational results with children. The present results strongly suggest that this assumption is tenuous. Given relatively similar sets of videotape conversations with children of different ethnic groups, there were interpretable differences in how teachers responded to these children. These differences were not solely predictable upon the basis of teacher race, but included further factors of pupil ethnicity, stereotyped attitudes, and the like. It is thought noteworthy that biases in the stereotypes could be associated in many cases with academic expectations in language arts expectancies.

A great number of research studies have consistently indicated that in any instructional situation, no matter what the status of the instructional materials and curriculum plan, the most salient variable is the teacher. If this is the case, then what we may find out about différences among teachers in terms of the way they perceive children, their stereotypes about them, and their academic expectations, may prove to be a most important factor not only in research, but in teacher recruitment, training, and job assignment.

chapter 5

MEASURING THE LATITUDE OF
LINGUISTIC ATTITUDES [1]

Introduction and Problem

One further main study done in the Texas project was devoted to the investigation of a revised method of scaling linguistic attitudes. Essentially the question was whether a linguistic attitude, rather than simply being represented as a "point" on a judgmental continuum or as plotted in a judgmental "space," might also have a dimension of breadth or latitude. For example, when a person is asked to evaluate the speech of a given child, perhaps his best estimate might be that the child sounds fairly confident, but that same evaluator might also be willing to indicate some range in that attitude. That is, he might rate the child as ranging from somewhat confident to very confident based on a range of behaviors that he experiences in the stimulus or what he might anticipate upon the basis of his stereotype. This concept of range of acceptable ratings is what we have referred to as *latitude of attitude.* This concept is not a new one, since a very similar question has been raised in the more general realm of attitude research by Sherif, Sherif and Nebergall (1965) in their social judgment-involvement approach to the study of attitudes. These theorists have maintained that a single point cannot adequately describe a person's attitude since an individual usually has a latitude of positions which he can accept. Particularly as applied to language attitudes, it is possible that a child may represent a particular range of confidence-eagerness and ethnicity-nonstandardness rather than single points on the judgmental continua. This leads to the use of scale options where a respondent may represent on a scale (such as below) what he would accept

[1] Research was conducted by Jack L. Whitehead and Frederick Williams with the assistance of Jean M. Civikly, Judi Witzke, and Maxine Streeter.

("latitude of acceptance") as a rating by a plus (+) and what he definitely would reject ("latitude of rejection") as a rating by a minus (-).

THE CHILD IS: passive__:__:__:__:__:__:__: active

Lack of decision, or "noncommitment" for any part of the scale would be indicated by a blank. Finally, the "best estimate" point on the scale would be indicated by circling one of the pluses. Essentially, the present research involved the application of this scaling technique to dialect attitude measurement.[2]

A final question was prompted by the extent to which personality characteristics might influence rating behavior. Sherif, Sherif, and Nebergall found that the size of the latitude of rejection was related to an individual's ego-involvement in the particular issue under investigation, with highly involved subjects rejecting more positions than moderately involved ones. Since one indicator of dogmatism is the magnitude of rejection of disbelief subsystems (Rokeach, 1960), it was thought that this personality variable could possibly be related to the way in which subjects marked the semantic differential scales.

In all, the questions of the study were:

1. What is the validity and reliability of the proposed scaling technique?
2. What is the relationship, if any, between the latitude of acceptance and the best estimate position, and between the latitude of acceptance and the latitude of rejection?
3. What is the relationship between measures of dogmatism and the size of the latitudes of acceptance, rejection, and noncommitment?

Method

Subjects

Participants in the study were 65 students enrolled in three sections of a freshman level course during the 1972 summer session at The University of Texas at Austin. All subjects were tested during regular classroom sessions and were told that their participation in the experiment would not affect their grades in the course.

Materials

Language samples consisted of one of the stimulus videotapes used in the earlier Texas research (Chapter 4). This type contained one lower- and one

---

[2]This approach is similar to one taken by C. David Mortensen and Kenneth K. Sereno, in "The Influence of Ego-Involvement and Discrepancy on Perceptions of Communication," *Speech Monographs*, 37 (June, 1970) 127-134.

middle-status child in each of the Anglo, Black, and Mexican-American ethnic groups.

Subjects were asked to respond to the children seen on tapes and to their average experiences with children of the three ethnic groups on ten semantic differential scales. These scales along with five filler scales comprised the evaluation form. The ten scales of interest in the study (which differ slightly from those in the Texas research reported in Chapter 4) were:

(Confidence-Eagerness)[3]
THE CHILD SEEMS: unsure—confident
THE CHILD IS: passive—active
THE CHILD SEEMS: reticent—eager to speak
THE CHILD SEEMS: hesitant—enthusiastic
THE CHILD SEEMS TO: dislike—like talking

(Ethnicity-Nonstandardness)
THE LANGUAGE OF THE CHILD'S HOME IS PROBABLY: marked ethnic style—standard American
THE CHILD SOUNDS: non-Anglo-like—Anglo-like
THE CHILD'S FAMILY IS PROBABLY: low—high social status
THE CHILD SEEMS CULTURALLY: disadvantaged—advantaged
THE CHILD'S SPEECH INDICATES: a poor educational background—a good one

These items, along with the five fillers, were randomly ordered in two parallel forms of the evaluation instrument.

The contrasting adjectives or phrases following each item were presented at either end of a seven-point scale. The scale mid-point was described as representative of a "neutral" or "don't know" rating, with the three positions on either side, moving out from the center, representing "slightly," "quite," and "very," with reference to the adjectives on each end.

Subjects were asked to complete the scales for each child or stereotype in the following manner: (1) by first placing a plus sign (+) on all scale positions which they believed they might possibly use to describe the child, (2) then circling the plus sign on the scale which they believed describes the child *best;* and (3) finally, by marking with a minus sign (-) all scale positions which they would definitely not use to describe the child. Subjects were also told that they might

---

[3]The adjective on the left indicates the pole of the scale assigned a value of 1.0 in the quantification scheme.

leave blank any scale positions for which they were unsure of their responses ("noncommitment").

During separate class sessions, a member of the research team who had not participated in gathering the ratings just described, went to each of the classes in the study and administered the Short Dogmatism Scale (Troldahl and Powell, 1965). A 20-item scale, the Short Dogmatism Scale, reduces by one-half the length of the original Dogmatism Scale, developed by Rokeach (1960), from which the former was taken. The 20 items selected for the short form include only those with item-total correlations of .30 or greater. The scale produces an approximated split-half reliability of .79, compared with .84 for the 40-item test. The shorter form correlates .94 with the original long form.

Procedures

Subjects completed the rating scales during regularly scheduled class periods during the first summer session of 1972 at The University of Texas at Austin. In each class, the regular instructors introduced the experimenters who explained to the class that they were involved in research concerning the use of videotape for instructional purposes and developing innovative scaling techniques. They asked the class for cooperation in trying out some of the new methods and assured them that their grades would not be affected in any way by their performance during the experimental sessions.

Before beginning the ratings, subjects completed a brief biographical inventory, requiring only name, age, classification, major, race, and previous teaching experience. They were assured that no personal identification would be used in the analysis and reporting of results.

Instructions were then given for completing the rating scales, and subjects were asked to fill out the first pages of scales by rating their "generalized idea of an Anglo child of about fourth-, fifth-, or sixth-grade level, based on their previous experience and knowledge, either direct or indirect." The same procedure was followed for generalized ratings of Black and Mexican-American children of the same age groups. Enough time was allowed for all subjects to complete the ratings before going on to the next, but subjects were encouraged to work as rapidly as possible. After these three ratings of groups were completed, the subjects were asked to watch the six videotapes of individual children, as previously described. Following each tape segment, subjects completed the fifteen scales for the child they had just seen.

Again, the dogmatism data were collected the following week by an experimenter whom students had not seen during the earlier rating session. The collection of this data was presented as unrelated to the work involving ratings.

Results

Preliminaries to the Analyses

One initial concern in preparing analyses in order to answer the main questions of the study was the degree to which the two-factor model of confidence-eagerness and ethnicity-nonstandardness was relevant under the revised condition of semantic differential administration. It was eventually concluded that the best check on this would be to determine the degree to which measures of the best estimate position if factored would result in the two-factor judgmental model. Such analysis was undertaken, and the results (Table 5.1) revealed the factor structure very similar to that found in our traditional use of the scales. The relevance of the two-factor model to the additional measures of amount of latitude of acceptance, rejection, and noncommitment may be seen in the subsequent description of answers to the first research question.

The results of the analyses will be discussed in accordance with each of the questions stated earlier.

TABLE 5.1

Factor Matrix of Ten Scales on the Best
Estimate Positions (Circled+)

Scales	Factor Loadings	
	I	II
1. unsure	.80	.23
2. passive	.75	.05
3. reticent	.87	.15
4. hesitant	.85	.18
5. dislike talking	.77	.13
6. marked ethnic style	.01	.83
7. non-Anglo-like	-.02	.85
8. low social status	.24	.80
9. disadvantaged	.32	.79
10. poor educational background	.35	.73
(Percentage total variance)	47.35%	21.43%

1. What Is the Validity and Reliability of the Proposed Technique?

It should be mentioned at the outset that one separate attempt to determine validity was unsuccessful, presumably for methodological reasons. It was an attempt to present pairs of tapes to listeners who then rated the average of the two children on a set of scales. It was anticipated that if the children in the two pairs were quite different, then the latitude of attitude measures would be much larger than if the pair of children were relatively similar. This attempt floundered mainly in meeting the assumption that listeners indeed would "average" judgments of two different children and as a consequence was discarded. In an alternative approach a more practical yet probably less objective method was employed. This involved calculating average ratings for the six different types of children and plotting these averages in a two-dimensional space. It was reasoned that validity could be argued to some degree by the extent to which the graphic plots differentiated among the children.

A computer program was designed which took into account the exact number of pluses, minuses, and blanks both to the left and to the right of the best estimate position on each scale. The program then summed the values of these items, calculated means, and then generated a graphic plot. In such plots, as shown in Figure 5.1, the average of the best estimate ratings for a child is

---

FIGURE 5.1

Two-factor graphic display of latitudes of acceptance (white area), rejection (dark area), noncommitment (grey area), and best estimate (the point) for Anglo children.

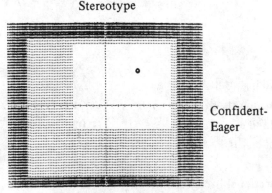

Stereotype

Confident-
Eager

Ethnic-Nonstandard

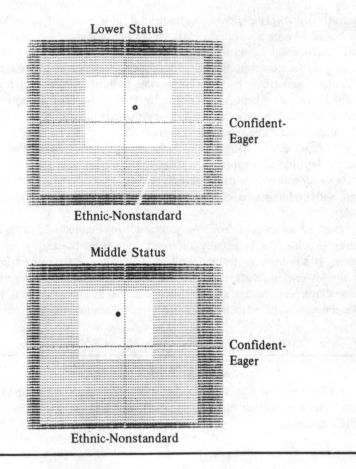

indicated by a " ∘ " on a two-dimensional plot of ethnicity-nonstandardness and confidence-eagerness. Then plotted about the two coordinates is an average amount of space indicative of ratings of the latitude of acceptance. These are shown in the present display as a nonmarked or white area. Next, surrounding the area of latitude of acceptance is an additional area of latitude of noncommitment which is shown in the grey space. Finally, shown in the darkest area, the two-factor space is exhausted by an indication of the latitude of rejection, the average of the two factors where minuses had been inserted on the scale. The present figures, then, not only indicate the locations of various aspects of acceptance, rejection and noncommitment, but also illustrate the relative size of each. The following discussion represents our interpretation of the graphic displays.

Ratings of Anglo children. As indicated in Figure 5.1, the middle-status Anglo child is generally rated as less ethnic and nonstandard than is the lower status Anglo child in terms of the best estimate (∘). In the case of these particular types however, there is not a very major differentiation in terms of confidence-eagerness; in fact, the lower-class child is rated slightly higher. It can be noted that the blank space reflecting the latitude of acceptance for the middle-class child is oriented in a more positive direction in the two-factor model than is the same space for the lower-status child. Further, ratings of the two videotapes can be compared with the ratings of the label of the stereotypes. Here, the latitude of acceptance is substantially larger than for either of the two videotapes, presumably because stereotypes would combine attitudes about both lower- and middle-status children and, as a consequence, would probably be broader.

Ratings of Black children. As indicated in Figure 5.2, ratings of Black children provide a substantially different plot from the ratings of the Anglo children. It has been typically found in studies using the same stimulus tapes that the lower-class Black child is rated ethnic and nonstandard and nonconfident and reticent, as against the higher status Black child being rated more confident-eager, but with a substantially more ethnic and nonstandard rating

---

FIGURE 5.2

Two-factor graphic display of latitudes of acceptance (white area), rejection (dark area), noncommitment (grey area), and best estimate (the point) for Black children.

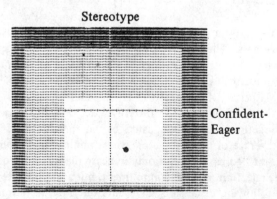

Stereotype

Confident-Eager

Ethnic-Nonstandard

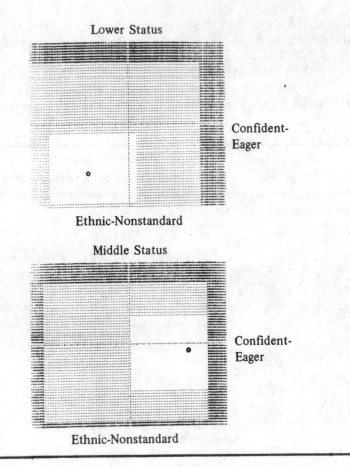

Lower Status

Confident-
Eager

Ethnic-Nonstandard

Middle Status

Confident-
Eager

Ethnic-Nonstandard

than his Anglo counterpart. Again, it can be seen that the area indicating latitude of acceptance generally distributes with the best estimate position. Different from the Anglo plots is the indication in Figure 5.2 that latitude of rejection indicates some relatively major difference according to Black children's status. In the case of the lower-status Black child, attitude rejection is concentrated at the nonethnic and standard end of the continuum. This generally indicates that the latitude of acceptance could be maximally indicative of ethnic-nonstandardness, since only a latitude of noncommitment separates it from the absolute perimeter of the model. Again, results indicate that the stereotype reaction for latitude of acceptance is considerably larger than that for rating the individual videotapes. This may also be an indication of how a stereotype takes into account to some degree status differences in the anticipation of variations in children. If the graphic plot for the Black children's stereotype is compared with the Anglo child's stereotype, it directly indicates the biases that are also found in the ratings of the videotapes of the Black children from the two status groups.

Ratings of Mexican-American children. Similar to the plots just discussed, the average ratings of the Mexican-American children (Figure 5.3) show a differentiation by status in terms of both confidence-eagerness and ethnicity-

---

FIGURE 5.3

Two-factor graphic display of latitudes of acceptance (white area), rejection (dark area), noncommitment (grey area), and best estimate (the point) for Mexican-American children.

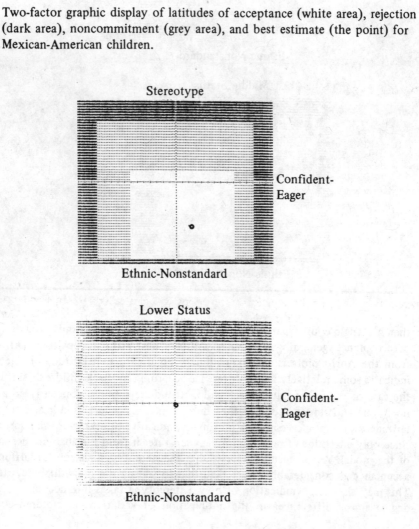

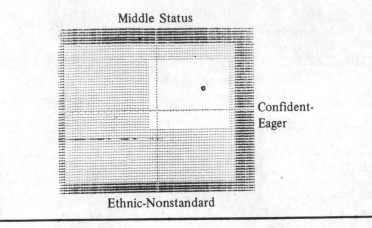

nonstandardness, with the middle-class child being rated more positively on both. Again, there is an indication of how the latitude of acceptance generally differentiates the children by status as does the best estimate rating. And again there is an indication—although less here than with the Anglo child—that latitude of acceptance for this stereotype will be considerably larger than that associated with particular videotapes.

Reliability. To assess the reliability of the present technique, intraclass correlations were calculated to determine both individual and average reliability of the instrument. Table 5.2 summarizes these reliabilities for each of the 14 variables. As can be seen from this table, the combined reliabilities were much higher than the individual reliabilities. Also it can be noted that reliabilities were higher when persons were rating the latitudes of acceptance, the latitudes of rejection and the best estimate positions, as particularly compared with the latitude of noncommitment. The results in this case are fairly straightforward: ratings of latitude of acceptance and latitude of rejection are relatively consistent, and hence their reliability could be assumed in research of this type.

2. What is the Relationship, If Any, Between the Latitude of Acceptance, and the Best Estimate Position, and Between the Latitude of Acceptance and the Latitude of Rejection?

Correlations were calculated between the latitude of acceptance and the best estimate position on each of the ten scales. These correlations were then converted to z-scores, averaged, and converted back to a correlation coefficient. The average correlation of mean of latitude of acceptance and the best estimate

TABLE 5.2

Intraclass Correlations of Subjects' Ratings

Variable	Confidence-Eagerness		Ethnicity-Nonstandardness	
	Individual	Average	Individual	Average
Size Lat. Acc.	.08	.85	.11	.89
Size Lat. Rej.	.14	.91	.12	.90
Size Lat. Non. Com.	.02	.55	.01	.36
Mean Lat. Acc.	.39	.98	.60	.99
Mean Lat. Rej.	.30	.96	.56	.99
Mean Lat. Non. Com.	.00	.20	.02	.52
Best Estimate	.42	.98	.64	.99

position was .85. The same procedure was repeated, this time using the latitude of acceptance and latitude of rejection correlations. The average correlation of the latitude of acceptance with the latitude of rejection was -.55.

In all, there seems to be a substantial relationship between the mean of the latitude of acceptance and the best estimate position and a lesser inverse relationship between the latitude of acceptance and the latitude of rejection.

3. What is the Relationship Between Measures of Dogmatism and the Size of the Latitude of Acceptance, Rejection, and Noncommitment?

As can be seen in Table 5.3, the correlations were quite weak, although some of them were statistically significant. The largest correlation was that between the size of the latitude of rejection on confidence-eagerness and dogmatism. The higher the dogmatism score, the larger the size of the latitude of rejection. We had expected that the more dogmatic an individual, the smaller would be his latitude of acceptance. However, the result of this analysis shows no significant

TABLE 5.3
Overall Correlations of 14 Variables
with Dogmatism Score

Variable	Correlation with Dogmatism	
	Confidence-Eagerness	Ethnicity-Nonstandardness
Size Lat. Acc.	-.055	-.077
Size Lat. Rej.	.142*	.114*
Size Lat. Non. Com.	-.117*	-.062
Mean Lat. Acc.	-.114*	-.068
Mean Lat. Rej.	.133*	.079
Mean Lat. Non. Com.	-.102*	-.135*
Best Estimate	-.112*	-.059

*$p < .05$.

relationship between an individual's dogmatism and the number of positions which he accepts or rejects on the two factors.

Discussion

The aim of the present research was to explore a method for measuring widths or latitudes of attitude in language evaluations. In all, the results generally indicated:

1. There is good evidence as to the validity and reliability of measures of best estimate, the latitudes of acceptance, rejection, and noncommitment. There should be, however, a more rigorous assessment made of the latitude measure per se. That is, there needs to be a more objective test involving independent measures of latitude of attitude and where the latitude of the phenomenon being judged is manipulated. Some evidence along this line was presented in the present study in that the stereotype latitudes of acceptance were generally larger than ratings of specific stimuli in the videotapes.

2. It appears as if measures of the best estimate position and the mid-point average of latitude of acceptance are very nearly the same thing. In a more theoretical vein, this indicates that a latitude of acceptance may be merely symmetrically distributed about the preferred position. The relatively lower inverse relationship between latitudes of acceptance and latitude of rejection indicates that one or the other varies; they do not necessarily draw from one another, but from the latitude of noncommitment.

3. There is no evidence whatsoever of a relationship between present measures of dogmatism and the various measures involved in the latitude of language attitudes.

Implications

It is the current opinion of the research team that the use of latitude measures presents a variety of interesting theoretical questions in the study of language attitudes. One of these is, of course, the degree to which amounts of latitude are somehow related to a person's expectancies concerning the speech of different types of children. An important extension of this same kind of question is the degree to which it might be possible to modify a person's stereotypes. Is it the case that the more experience a person has with linguistic diversity and a particular group of children, the larger will be his latitude of acceptance? If, indeed, it is possible to modify the degree of latitude of acceptance, does this typically draw from the latitude of noncommitment, or the latitude of rejection? Perhaps change in the latitude of linguistic attitudes is a result of a more primary change in the reduction of latitude of rejection. At best, the present two-factor graphic model could be used for research which attempts to determine how linguistic attitudes might be manipulated.

The present models enter somewhat into the line of speculation as to how linguistic attitudes may be elicited in any given situation of judgment. Perhaps, when a respondent is involved in a particular act of judging, he responds to only a few initial cues at first which elicit in his mind the stereotype of children of that type. Then, it is with reference to this stereotype that the particular child is judged. In terms of the present two-factor model, perhaps the best estimate rating given of a particular stereotype is the hub about which any given child's videotape may be rated. As such, then the speculation would also suggest that the latitude of attitude in the stereotype measures would represent the space within which a particular child might be judged. Put another way, there is a high probability that a child of any particular type would be judged within the space of a person's latitude of attitude as indicated on the stereotype plot of the child.

There should be less probability of his being judged acceptable in the range of noncommitment and almost no probability of his being judged within the latitude of rejection. Again, the present model may serve not only a heuristic but a direct research measurement function in the studies along this line.

chapter 6

A SUMMARY OF RELATED PROJECTS

Introduction

We conclude this monograph with a collection of reports of further studies which in a variety of ways represent appendages of the research in the Chicago and Texas projects. These projects were suggested in the course of planning the major studies or were prompted by the findings of one of those studies. In overview, the studies to be described are as follows:

Regional variations in "sounding disadvantaged." Using the same language samples as were administered in the Chicago study, Williams and Shamo (1972) compared ratings of the Chicago teachers on the scale "sounding disadvantaged" with ratings by teachers in Memphis, Tennessee.

Ethnic guise. Ethnic stereotyping was further studied by Williams, Whitehead, and Miller (1971b) in a design where ratings of the same standard English audio samples were compared when matched with varying video images of a Black, White, and Mexican-American child.

Dialect switching. A study by Williams and Miller (1971) examined the effects of dialect switching of a mature Black and a Mexican-American speaker relative to ratings of both of these speakers in terms of language and personality traits.

Employer evaluations of speech. Hopper and Williams (1973) employed a semantic differential scaling approach to assess interviewers' attitudes toward speech representative of prospective employees. Such attitudes were then used in an attempt to predict hiring decisions.

Regional Variations in Teacher Attitudes
Toward Children's Language[1]

One key question arising in the Chicago study was the generality of association between the speech characteristics and social stereotyping to other regions of the country. The present study represented one partial attempt to answer this question by the comparison of selected ratings of these same children as obtained from southern teachers (Memphis, Tennessee) with the ratings obtained earlier from northern teachers. A further objective was to compare the degree to which characteristics of the children's speech could predict ratings of "culturally advantaged—disadvantaged."

Method

The stimulus materials and semantic differential scales were the same ones as described in the Chicago study (Chapter 3). Eighty-seven teachers (54 Blacks, 33 White) were volunteers in the study. They represented elementary schools in a Memphis school district which ranged from all Black, to mixed, to predominantly White schools. These teachers were tested within the context of an in-service training day for the school district. Teachers' tape rating sessions were conducted as closely as possible according to the same procedures as in the earlier study. For purposes of the present analyses, the data included (1) the teachers' responses to the scales as used in the Chicago research, including the scale of culturally advantaged—disadvantaged, (2) the differentiation of Black and White teacher raters, and (3) the differentiation of stimulus tapes according to child characteristics. Parallel data of this same type were available from the Chicago study.

Results and Discussion

Factor structure. Initial analyses (not reported in the Williams and Shamo, 1972, article) indicated the presence of a two-factor model of confidence-eagerness and ethnicity-nonstandardness. However, no comparisons between northern and southern teachers were made at the time because the interest then was to determine if ratings of being "culturally advantaged—disadvantaged" would differ. In short, the two-factor model held, but no attempt was made to determine if the groups of teachers rated the children differently *within* the model.

Sounding "disadvantaged." Responses to this scale were quantified by assigning the value "1" to the disadvantaged pole, then numbering the cells to

---

[1] This research appears in more detail in Williams and Shamo (1972).

the opposite extreme of "advantaged." These quantified scale ratings then served as a dependent variable in a five-way analysis of variance, with dimensions corresponding to teacher ethnicity, region of the study, the child's social status, the child's ethnicity, and the child's sex (topic was subsumed). Results of the overall analysis are next summarized.

1. There were no statistically significant overall differences in the ratings of advantaged–disadvantaged according to the regions of the teachers (means: northern = 4.0, southern = 3.9). Neither were there any significant interactions involving the region variable with any of the other dimensions in the analysis. This indicated that results generally were consistent for ratings of teachers in the northern and southern samples.

2. The only significant (p <.05) variation involving teacher ethnicity was in the interaction of teacher ethnicity and child ethnicity. Differences among the means in this interaction indicated that White teachers tended to rate White children as slightly more culturally advantaged (mean equals 4.6) than did Black teachers (4.3). Additionally, although Black children were generally rated as more "culturally disadvantaged" than White children, White teachers tended to rate them more so (3.3) than did Black teachers (3.7). (This has been found also in both the Chicago and Texas studies.)

3. A significant (p <.05) three-way interaction among child status, race, and sex accounted for the only differences involving these three variables. In general, and as anticipated, children sampled from middle-status families were typically rated more culturally advantaged (4.3) than those from low-status families (3.5). The chief contrast, however, was that status differences were found more for Black children than for White ones. This difference was the most marked of all in the differentiation of middle-status Black female children (4.8) as contrasted with low-status Black female children (2.6). White middle-status males were rated as more advantaged (4.5) than their lower-status counterparts (3.9). For White females, however, this was a status reversal in the ratings (middle = 4.3, low = 4.9). While status differences generally prevailed, the magnitude of the difference varied according to sex and ethnicity of the child.

It should again be noted that the lack of a significant interaction of these variables with teacher ethnicity or teacher region, indicated that these patterns had generality across those two variables.

Regional differences in the prediction of ratings. As already mentioned, the stimulus tapes had been assessed for a variety of characteristics which were used as predictors of scale ratings in the northern study. Sixteen of those characteristics are listed in Table 6.1 along with their partial correlations in predicting ratings of a child's sounding culturally advantaged–disadvantaged. An

TABLE 6.1

Partial Correlations of Predictor Variables Obtained from
Regression Equations of Ratings of "Cultural Disadvantage"
upon Sample Characteristics

Variables	Teachers			
	Northern		Southern	
	Black	White	Black	White
Silent pauses	-.38*	-.34*	-.26*	-.39*
Filled pauses	-.04	-.20	-.18	-.21
Junctures per utterance	.17	.15	.10	.19
Utterance total	.10	.07	.14	-.08
Clause ratio	.06	.26*	.05	.28*
Sentence length	.06	.25*	.19	.38*
Verb construction	.08	.25*	.06	.15
Introductory interj.	.21*	.33*	.27*	.32*
Pronominal apposition	-.30*	-.17	-.31*	-.19
Deviations in main verb	-.13	-.27*	-.34*	-.30*
[-s] or [-z] deviations	-.08	-.21	-.33*	-.16
[ɵ] or [ð] deviations	-.26*	-.23	-.43*	-.38*
[-t] or [-d] deviations	-.23*	.04	.00	-.11
[m] deviations	-.21*	-.20	-.17	-.23
[n] deviations	-.15	-.22	-.07	-.27
[ŋ] deviations	-.02	-.12	-.10	-.22
Child's race	-.18*	-.50*	-.23*	-.51*
Multiple *R* from regression equation =	(.66)	(.72)	(.73)	(.70)

*Variables included in a seven variable prediction equation.

additional variable among these correlates is an identification of the child's race, treated as a binary variable. The larger the correlation between the race and the ratings, the more it indicates that a child from a particular race is likely to be rated either high or low on the scale. Footnotes with the partial correlations indicate those variables that were included in the optimum multiple regression equation of the ratings of cultural advantage—disadvantage upon the array of predictor variables. By examination of the partial correlations given in Table 6.1, it is possible to compare the northern and southern teachers in terms of which tape stimulus characteristics best predicted the ratings of culturally advantaged—disadvantaged. Further it is possible to compare teachers by ethnic subgroups. Some generalizations derived from examination of this table are as follows:

1. The ratings by all teachers, whether Black or White, northern or southern, can be partly predicted by the number of silent pauses in the children's tape. The negative correlation of this variable indicates that the fewer times a child hesitates in his sample, the less he was rated as culturally disadvantaged, or vice versa.

2. The ratings of White teachers, both northern and southern, but not Black teachers, seem to be partly predictable from the use of clauses and their lengths in relation to sentence fragments or nonsentences. As a child tended to use more clauses relative to fragments, and his sentences tended to be longer, he was rated as more culturally advantaged. Measures of the complexity of verb construction tended toward this same pattern; however, they were a salient predictor variable only in the case of White northern teachers' ratings.

3. The use of introductory interjections (e.g., "Anyhow . . . ") are partial predictors for all teachers' ratings of a child sounding culturally advantaged—disadvantaged. The more the child used such interjections, the more he was rated toward the culturally advantaged end of the scale.

4. The ratings by Black teachers, both northern and southern, but not White teachers, tended to be partly predicted by the incidence of the grammatical nonstandardization known as pronominal apposition ("The man *he* came home."). By contrast the ratings by all except northern Black teachers tended also to be partly predicted by nonstandardizations in the main verb. In all, it appears as if such grammatical nonstandardizations are salient predictors of ratings of being culturally disadvantaged, although perhaps more so for the ratings by Black teachers than for the White teachers.

5. Among the various phonological nonstandardizations, the variations in the realization of voiced and voiceless *th* sounds (ð, θ) tended to be the best predictors of ratings of cultural advantage—disadvantage. Viewed in terms of type of teachers, predictions of ratings from different phonological variables seem to be found most within the group of northern Black teachers. In all cases, nonstandardizations, as would be expected, had a negative correlation with ratings of being culturally advantaged.

6. The partial correlation of a child's race with ratings of culturally advantaged–disadvantaged indicated a marked contrast between the ratings of Black teachers and White teachers. The correlations clearly show that if a child is to be judged on this scale, his ratings by White teachers will typically be more toward culturally disadvantaged than his ratings by Black teachers.

In summary, analysis of linguistic cues indicate that even after very short exposure to a child's speech, Chicago and Memphis Black and White teacher judgments tended to classify a child as being "culturally disadvantaged" if his verbal and grammatical patterns were not standard or if his speech was hesitant. This was especially true if his speech exhibited irregularities in grammar, silent pausing, and pronunciation. This stereotype was extended by the fact that such associations were also significantly related to child race.

Ethnic Stereotyping and Judgments of Children's Speech[2]

As noted in Chapter 3, some teachers in the Chicago study were "incorrect" in rating the speech of particular children. Subsequently research by Naremore found that, to some degree, teachers could be grouped in terms of their commonality in rating Black children as compared to White ones. The major implication of that series of analyses was that teachers' stereotypes of children from particular ethnic groups may have been playing a key role in the process of speech rating.

The present research was an effort to assess the effects of ethnic stereotyping in a design where ratings of the same standard English audio samples could be compared when alternatively matched with the video image of a White, Black, or Mexican-American child. If ethnic stereotyping affects speech ratings, we should expect that (1) the ratings of the same audiotape language samples will differ in these various video-image conditions, and (2) the direction of difference will be biased toward stereotyped ratings of the minority group children.

Method

Materials. Four videotapes were prepared for the present research: one each of a Black and a Mexican-American child, and two of White children, all of lower social status families. Each tape was a 90-second segment showing a side view of a child assembling a plastic model car. The child was describing his actions and discussing what he would do with his new car. Slight lip movement

---

[2]This research appears in more detail in Williams, Whitehead, and Miller (1971b).

in the video segments was detectable but insufficient for lip-reading by viewers. For purposes of the testing design, two "ethnic guise" versions of each of the minority group children were prepared by using the audio tracks from the standard-English-speaking White children. For each of the Black and Mexican-American children's videotapes, there was the original version with a nonstandard English audio track, then two additional versions each with one of the standard English audio recordings paired with it. The same set of semantic differential scales were used as from the Central Texas study.

Subjects. Listener-evaluators were 44 undergraduate education majors (42 females, 2 males) enrolled in a speech course for prospective elementary teachers at The University of Texas.

Procedure. Two weeks prior to the videotape presentations, subjects completed a pre-test response booklet consisting of (1) an explanation of the session under the guise of a two-part experiment designed to determine the correspondence of teachers' evaluations of children's language with evaluations made by a standardized test battery; (2) instructions for completing the semantic differential; and (3) three evaluation forms requesting ratings of a "Black Child," "Anglo Child," and "Mexican-American Child," based upon the person's average experiences with them. These ratings were considered (by the researchers) to index stereotype evaluations.

For the videotape ratings, subjects were tested in groups of five or six persons in a small conference room utilizing an 11-inch television monitor. Each group viewed (1) a Black or Mexican-American child whose nonstandard speech had been replaced by dubbing in the speech of a standard-English-speaking child, (2) a Black or Mexican-American child speaking nonstandard English, and (3) a White child speaking standard English. Each subject saw either the Black or Mexican-American child in the standard English version, but not both.

Results

Differences among the standard English samples. To answer the first question of whether differences among the standard English audio samples would be found as these samples appeared with the ethnic guise conditions, response data were cast into two-way analysis of variance models. Independent variables were the two standard English audio samples and the three videotape conditions of the White, Black, and Mexican-American children. The two analysis models were for the separate dependent variables—factor scores of confidence-eagerness and of ethnicity-nonstandardness.

The analysis of confidence-eagerness ratings revealed a significant main effect on the ethnicity variable ($F = 9.5$, $df = 2/82$, $p < .001$), and a significant main effect for the two different standard English samples ($F = 11.6$, $df = 1/82$, $p <$

TABLE 6.2

Mean Ratings of Standard English Audio
Samples As Paired with Video Images

Factor	Videotape Ethnic Condition		
	Caucasian	Black	Mexican-American
Confidence-eagerness	23.1_a*	22.2_a	18.4_b
Ethnicity-nonstandardness	30.1_a	21.8_b	21.1_b

*For comparisons within rows, means with common subscripts are not significantly different ($p < .05$) from one another by Duncan range tests.

.001). There was no significant interaction. As shown in Table 6.2, results of comparisons among the means of the three levels of the ethnic factor revealed that standard English tapes paired with Mexican-American children were rated significantly ($p < .05$) lower on confidence-eagerness than were pairings with White or Black children. The latter two were not significantly different from each other.

Differences not shown between the two standard English audio samples indicated that one tape was consistently rated higher (22.8) than the other (19.8) but that this did not interact significantly with the pattern of differences found for the ethnic guise conditions.

Results of the analysis of ethnicity-nonstandardness ratings revealed a significant main effect on the ethnicity dimension ($F = 31.8$, $df = 2/82$, $p < .001$). No significant effect due to the two audio sample tapes nor an interaction were found. Comparisons among the individual means for the ethnic guise conditions indicated that pairings with Mexican-American and Black children were rated as more ethnic-nonstandard than pairings with the White children. Again, there was no significant difference between the two standard English tapes. (means = 24.8, 23.9).

Evidence of stereotype biases. The question whether biases among the ethnic guise conditions could be associated with stereotyping led to the comparison of ethnic guise ratings with ratings obtained in responses to the ethnic labels. Here the assumption was that the ratings of "average" experience with children of different ethnicities would serve as a stereotype index. A secondary comparison was also possible between the guise conditions and videotapes with the original nonstandard English audio samples. Analyses involved direct t-test comparisons of cell means.[3]

Mean confidence-eagerness ratings, of children obtained in the stereotype evaluations (labels) (White 23.6, Black 20.3, Mexican-American 18.4), did not differ significantly from the comparable means (Table 6.2) obtained from the videotapes of the three ethnic groups which all had standard English audio samples. Nor were there differences between the ratings of minority child videotapes with the children speaking nonstandard English (Black 20.6, Mexican-American 16.5) or when standard English had been dubbed in place of the original speech.

Although there was no significant difference between label ratings of ethnicity-nonstandardness based on labels of children identified as "Anglo" (30.0) and the corresponding videotape (Table 6.2), the label ratings of "Black" (12.5) and "Mexican-American" (12.0) were significantly lower than the corresponding ethnic guise conditions. Similar significant differences were found in the comparisons of the videotapes having nonstandard English audio samples (Black 14.6, Mexican-American 12.4) with the same minority group children with standard English dubbed in. Thus while the standard English samples paired with Black and Mexican-American children in the ethnic guise condition were rated more nonstandard and ethnic than when paired with a White child's videotape, the bias was substantially short of both the stereotype index (label ratings) and the ratings of the minority group children with their actual sound tracks.

Discussion

In general, findings indicated that the videotape image showing the child's ethnicity affects ratings of his language in the direction of racial stereotyping expectations. For Black children the bias was in the direction of expecting them to sound more nonstandard and ethnic than their White peers. For Mexican-American children, the bias was not only toward expecting greater ethnicity-nonstandardness but also more reticence and nonconfidence. An obvious restriction of these findings is to the types of children and teacher candidates studied.

---

[3]So as not to reveal the ethnic guise combinations, only one guise was used per subject. This complicated the testing design such that only the overall comparisons of the primary results could be subjected to analysis of variance efficiently. Remaining mean comparisons were best made by individual t-tests which were interpreted for statistical significance at the $p < .05$ level.

The question arises as to whether the subjects might have responded simply to the visual image alone or whether the audio track was influencing judgment of the children. In ratings of confidence-eagerness there appears to be no difference in ratings of children when speaking standard and nonstandard English. However, in the case of ethnicity-nonstandardness it is clear from comparisons of the ethnic guise ratings with ratings of videotapes having their original nonstandard English audio tracks that teacher candidates were differentiating children based, in part at least, upon characteristics of the audio track.

The present research indicated that linguistic cues were not carefully attended to for the minority group children in the ethnic guise conditions and suggested that the visual cues of ethnicity either biased the perceptions of the language cues or simply made them irrelevant to the evaluator. Cue irrelevance seemed to be the case for confidence-eagerness ratings where the stereotype (label) ratings and ethnic guise ratings corresponded closely. However, on ratings of ethnicity-nonstandardness the bias in ethnic guise ratings was only in the direction of the stereotype, rather than fitting the stereotype itself. This suggested that evaluators may not simply report their stereotypes when rating children's language, but may interpret the language cues which are biased partly by their stereotyped expectations.

If ethnocentrism is involved in the stereotype effects found in the present research, then it should be possible to test ways of countering it. For example, subjects such as in the present study could be given extensive videotape experiences in a particular variety of dialect contrasts. The ethnic guise technique could then be employed to test whether they have become more sensitive to what they hear in a language sample and less influenced by stereotyped expectations.

Effects of Dialect Switching on Language and Personality Evaluations[4]

The attitudes which listeners associate with various dialects, of course, depends upon the background of the respondent and what he knows of the circumstances of the speech situation. In the present study an attempt was made to contrast language and personality attitudes associated with standard English dialect against Black and Spanish-influenced dialects of English, all in a conversational situation. The respondents in this case were Anglo-American college students, none of whom spoke other than the so-called standard dialect.

The central research question was whether these respondents would make consistent and interpretable attitudinal differentiations between the samples of

---

[4]This research has not been previously published.

Black English and standard English obtained from a female Black speaker, and between standard English and Spanish-influenced English as obtained from a Mexican-American male speaker. The respondents were not informed that the dialect comparisons in these cases were from the same speakers. The basic vocabulary and sentence construction in all language samples was held constant.

Method

Materials. As part of a prior research project, written transcripts were available of conversational responses to the following three questions: (1) Would you rather be rich or poor? (2) Would you rather live in a big city or small town? (3) Would you like to go to the moon? For the present research, the initial 90 seconds (approximately 120 words) of each of these answers formed the content of speech samples that were to be obtained in standard English dialect and in versions of Black and Spanish-influenced English. Two speakers, both available from an ongoing program of dialect study, were instructed to practice reading aloud these transcripts, one version in standard English (which they were already known to speak) and one version in an alternative dialect (in which they were also known to be proficient). The researchers observed the practice sessions, and when the dialect versions appeared to fit most of the well-known distinctions between standard English and Black English, or standard English and Spanish-influenced English, tape recordings were made. Among characteristics of the Spanish-influenced English were occasional rising inflection at the end of sentences, substitution of "ch" [c] for "sh" [s], "s" for "z," and a long /i/ for short /I/ as in rēch for rich. The Black female's Black dialect version was marked by vowel lengthening, deletion of final consonants, change in intonation pattern, and a more rapid rate of utterances compared to the standard English version. In addition, four other speakers (two females, two males) were asked to record standard English versions. These merely served as filler materials which were randomized in testing with the four dialect versions but were not considered in the analysis. Of concern, then, were four stimulus segments per topic—viz., one for each of the two speakers' standard English versions, and one for each of the dialect versions.

One portion of the rating instrument consisted of semantic differential scales as used for the two-factor judgmental model of *confidence-eagerness* and *ethnicity-nonstandardness.* The second portion was comprised of 14 scales, drawn from research by Lambert *et al.* (1960), and used to measure personal characteristics. Each characteristic was gauged as follows:

KINDNESS:
     very little __ : __ : __ : __ : __ : __ : __ very much

The thirteen additional terms were sense of humor, dependability, intelligence, likability, leadership, sociability, self-confidence, height, good looks, ambition, character, entertainingness, and religiousness. Ten language attitude scales were randomly mixed with the fourteen personality scales and three filler scales to form the rating instrument for the study.

Subjects. Forty-five undergraduate students enrolled in School of Communication courses at The University of Texas participated as volunteers in the experiment. Most were sophomores and juniors, and all were Anglo.

Procedures. Subjects were randomly assigned to, and tested in, three groups of fifteen in a conference room. The study was presented under the guise of judging people's personality from their voices. Subjects were led to believe that objective personality measures were available for the persons they would hear and that after rating them they would be able to compare their ratings with the objective measures. Each subject was provided a booklet consisting of a cover sheet explaining the purpose of the experiment, directions on how to complete the semantic differential scales, and eight evaluation forms. All subjects were played eight audiotape samples (four filler voices and the four dialect versions) in a randomized sequence and were allowed time to complete the evaluation form after hearing each segment. However, each of the three groups heard a different topic. Before being dismissed from the experiment, all subjects were debriefed.

Data tabulation. Scale quantification was accomplished by assigning a one to seven value. A factor analysis of the ten scales used in language attitude rating revealed, as expected, the existence of the confidence-eagernes and ethnicity-nonstandardness factors. Factor scores were calculated as the sum of the five scales for each factor. Personality ratings were directly quantified on a one to seven scale, beginning with the "very little" pole of the scale.

Results

Language attitudes. The principal focus in analysis of language attitudes was differences between dialect conditions for each speaker within topics. A method of planned comparisons was employed using a three-way (topic × speaker × dialect) analysis of variance model, and Scheffé tests. Table 6.3 summarizes the subsets of mean scores for the language attitude measures.

One pattern which appears for confidence-eagerness ratings is that the Black and Mexican-American speakers were judged as more confident and eager when speaking in their primary dialect than when speaking in standard English. This held on all three topics. Another generalization was that the Black speaker speaking Black English was always judged as more confident-eager than any other of the tapes in the respective subsets.

TABLE 6.3
Means of Language Attitude Ratings

Topic/Attitude/Speaker	Dialect	
	Standard English	Alternate Dialect
(1) being rich or poor		
Confidence-eagerness		
Black	23.8_b*	26.6_c
Mexican-American	14.9_a	21.3_b
Ethnicity-nonstandardness		
Black	22.5_a	26.8_b
Mexican-American	21.1_a	27.0_b
(2) living in a city or town		
Confidence-eagerness		
Black	15.6_{ab}	26.0_c
Mexican-American	13.5_a	17.1_b
Ethnicity-nonstandardness		
Black	23.7_b	24.8_{ab}
Mexican-American	19.2_a	25.8_c
(3) going to the moon		
Confidence-eagerness		
Black	14.1_a	31.4_d
Mexican-American	18.8_b	23.8_c
Ethnicity-nonstandardness		
Black	23.5_{ab}	21.8_b
Mexican-American	18.1_a	24.3_c

*Means with common subscripts within topic-attitude-speaker subsets are not significantly ($p < .05$) different from each other.

The comparisons of alternative dialects on ratings of ethnicity-nonstandardness (Table 6.3) revealed more consistent differences for the Mexican-American speaker than for the Black. Results, however, were generally in the direction of the nonstandard version being rated as more ethnic-nonstandard (as expected, of course). The pattern among these same means

TABLE 6.4

Means of Personality Scale Ratings

Scale	Speaker: Dialect:	Mexican-American SE	NSE	Black SE	NSE
Sense of humor		3.0	4.2*	3.2	5.5*
Dependable		4.1	3.9	3.9	4.0
Intelligence		3.9	3.6	3.6	3.4
Likability		4.3	5.0	4.0	5.4*
Kindness		4.3	5.1	4.5	5.0
Leadership		3.1	3.4	3.6	3.3
Sociability		3.3	4.1	3.8	4.5
Self-Confidence		3.1	4.2*	3.8	5.4*
Height		3.9	3.6	4.3	4.2
Good Looks		3.8	3.6	3.8	3.9
Ambition		3.7	4.0	3.9	4.2
Character		3.8	4.4	4.1	5.1*
Entertainingness		3.1	4.2*	3.2	5.1*
Religiousness		4.5	4.7	4.4	4.7

*Dialect versions for the same speaker have significantly ($p < .05$) different mean ratings.

further suggested that the differences were mainly due to the Mexican speaker's standard English being rated less nonstandard than the Black speaker's standard English.

Personality ratings. Planned comparisons were also used to examine differences in the personality ratings; this involved an analysis of variance for each of the fourteen variables. The general lack of interactions with topic differences led to summing across this variable. Also, since sex differences could confound dialect comparisons between speakers, comparisons were only made within speakers' dialect alternatives. These comparisons are summarized in Table 6.4.

A major generalization was that wherever significant differences did exist between two dialect versions for the speaker, it was typically in terms of a more favorable rating for the alternative dialect than for standard English. A second generalization was that there were more differentiations between the dialects of the Black speaker than the Mexican-American. In particular, all three of the personality differentiations for the dialects of the Mexican-American were also found between the dialects of the Black speaker. These were *sense of humor, self-confidence,* and *entertainingness.* The additional personality distinctions between the dialects of the Black speaker were on ratings of *likability* and *character.*

Discussion

A problem in studies of the present type is the question of how far results may be generalized relative to topics, speakers, attitudes, and particularly raters. The language and personality ratings used in the present study have a known generality across a series of studies. It can be argued, too, that the major characteristics of the dialects studied in this research have a fair degree of generality across groups of speakers. The consistency of most attitude measures across the topics in the present study give some evidence of generality, but it is nevertheless sparse. Finally, we are most severely limited by the types of raters used in this study.

Given these restrictions, however, there appeared to be several noteworthy generalizations which can be drawn from the present results. First, there seems to be good evidence that, similar to the Lambert research with Canadian French-English bilinguals, distinctions in personality ratings will be reliably made between the two dialects of functionally bidialectical Mexican-American or Black speakers. That these personality ratings can be associated with a conscious perception of language differences was shown by the consistent differences in the language attitude measures.

A second generalization is that the differences in personality ratings which favored the alternative dialects to standard English may reflect more negatively upon the speaker's use of standard English than they do favorably upon the alternative dialects. Recall in the language attitude rating that the differences between the two dialects in terms of ethnicity-nonstandardness were not as consistent nor as great as the differences in terms of confidence-eagerness. It appeared that noteworthy differences were evident in the standard English version being rated as less confident-eager. In prior research (Williams, 1970b), ratings of confidence-eagerness have been predicted from the incidence of hesitation phenomena, or lack of fluency, in particular. Speculation here is that the speakers may have sounded simply more at ease and natural and were thus more fluent when speaking a primary dialect than when speaking in the standard English version. It should be remembered that these transcripts were of conversational speech, and such speech is not the style that typically requires standard English, particularly in bidialectical speakers of these types. It may be, then, that if a bidialectical speaker uses his primary dialect in conversational situations such as the present one, he will generally be perceived more favorably by an audience of the type studied here than if there is an attempt to speak in standard English. All this is, of course, speculation, but it does indicate that using a primary and nonstandard dialect in speech situations such as represented in this study may not be as unfavorable as many speech and English teachers have presumed. Furthermore, although it could be argued that given ratings such as in job interviews, one might not expect the results to be as favorable to nonstandard dialects; as the next study demonstrates, employers also may be more interested in other factors than ethnicity and standardness of dialect.

Speech Characteristics and Employability[5]

The present research focused upon relationships between employers' attitudes toward speech samples and the employers' hiring decisions with regard to the speakers. The thesis was that an interviewee's speech characteristics furnish cues which form employer's attitudes toward the speaker. These attitudes influence employment decisions.

Using semantic differential techniques, the present researchers attempted to ascertain dimensions of employers' judgments of speech of prospective employees and to relate these judgments to hiring decisions relative to the speakers.

Study I: Scale Development

Method. Subjects were professional employment interviewers—persons who, as part of their regular job routines, conducted employment interviews and made hiring decisions. A total of 76 employers participated in the study. They were contacted by telephoning organizations listed in an Austin, Texas, Chamber of Commerce document as employing 200 or more persons.

The researchers consulted with several personnel interviewers to ascertain "typical" questions asked during job interviews. Questions were selected which were deemed likely to elicit extensive responses from interviewees, and which contained no references to particular job categories. Selected questions (for example: "How do you go about solving a problem at work?" "What is your concept of the ideal boss?") were asked of adult males from the Central Texas area. Their responses were tape-recorded and edited into 90-second segments.

---

[5]This research is also reported by Hopper and Williams (1973), and Hopper, *et al.* (1972).

Four 90-second recordings were played for twelve employment interviewers. After each recording, interviewers were asked to describe their reactions to the speech which had been recorded. Field workers copied all descriptive terms used by the employers. Employers were also asked to indicate whether or not the tapes sounded like a "real job interview." Ten of twelve respondents indicated that the recordings were realistic representations of employment interviews.

Given the adjectives supplied by employers, a set of forty semantic differential scales (Table 6.5) was constructed. Also, a set of five-point scales was developed for employers to indicate the probability that they would hire the person being interviewed for each of seven job categories—executive, public relations, foreman, skilled technician, sales, clerical, and manual labor. Possible responses ranged from "definitely would hire" to "definitely would not hire." Thus the test instrument measured the employer's perception of the interviewee's speech and the probability that he would actually employ the speaker.

Twenty-three employers were then asked to respond on the test instrument to 90-second samples of simulated interviews for each of four speakers. The speakers were a Black, a Mexican-American, a White southern, and a standard English speaker.

TABLE 6.5
Scales Used to Index the Two-Factor
Model in Study One

THE SPEAKER SOUNDS:
   limited __ : __ : __ : __ : __ : __ : __ versatile*

THE SPEAKER SOUNDS:
   *confident __ : __ : __ : __ : __ : __ : __ unsure

THE SPEAKER:
   has problems communicating __ : __ : __ : __ : __ : __ : __ communicates
                                                                       well*

THE SPEAKER SOUNDS:
   cold __ : __ : __ : __ : __ : __ : __ warm

THE SPEAKER SOUNDS:
   disadvantaged __ : __ : __ : __ : __ : __ : __ advantaged*

THE SPEAKER SOUNDS:
   hard to understand __ : __ : __ : __ : __ : __ : __ easy to understand*

TABLE 6.5 (continued)

THE SPEAKER SOUNDS:
    hesitant __ : __ : __ : __ : __ : __ : __ fluent*

THE SPEAKER SOUNDS:
    *Anglo-like __ : __ : __ : __ : __ : __ : __ non-Anglo-like

THE SPEAKER'S BACKGROUND IS:
    different from mine __ : __ : __ : __ : __ : __ : __ like mine*

THE SPEAKER SOUNDS:
    lazy __ : __ : __ : __ : __ : __ : __ short

THE SPEAKER SOUNDS:
    *eager __ : __ : __ : __ : __ : __ : __ reticent

THE SPEAKER SOUNDS:
    *interested __ : __ : __ : __ : __ : __ : __ uninterested

THE SPEAKER SOUNDS:
    *calm __ : __ : __ : __ : __ : __ : __ frightened

THE SPEAKER SOUNDS:
    *cooperative __ : __ : __ : __ : __ : __ : __ uncooperative

THE SPEAKER SOUNDS:
    *casual __ : __ : __ : __ : __ : __ : __ formal

THE SPEAKER SOUNDS:
    *dependable __ : __ : __ : __ : __ : __ : __ undependable

THE SPEAKER SOUNDS:
    *educated __ : __ : __ : __ : __ : __ : __ uneducated

THE SPEAKER SOUNDS:
    *fast __ : __ : __ : __ : __ : __ : __ slow

THE SPEAKER SOUNDS:
    *enthusiastic __ : __ : __ : __ : __ : __ : __ lacking in enthusiasm

THE SPEAKER SOUNDS:
    repetitive __ : __ : __ : __ : __ : __ : __ concise*

THE SPEAKER SOUNDS:
    old __ : __ : __ : __ : __ : __ : __ young*

TABLE 6.5 (continued)

THE SPEAKER SOUNDS:
    disorganized __ : __ : __ : __ : __ : __ : __ organized*

THE SPEAKER SOUNDS:
    evasive __ : __ : __ : __ : __ : __ : __ straightforward*

THE SPEAKER:
    uses many words __ : __ : __ : __ : __ : __ : __ uses few words*

THE SPEAKER SOUNDS:
    *thorough __ : __ : __ : __ : __ : __ : __ superficial

THE SPEAKER HAS A:
    bad voice __ : __ : __ : __ : __ : __ : __ good voice*

THE SPEAKER'S TONE IS:
    even __ : __ : __ : __ : __ : __ : __ varied*

THE SPEAKER SOUNDS:
    *cheerful __ : __ : __ : __ : __ : __ : __ sad

THE SPEAKER:
    *expresses himself well __ : __ : __ : __ : __ : __ : __ poorly

THE SPEAKER SOUNDS:
    *relaxed __ : __ : __ : __ : __ : __ : __ tense

THE SPEAKER SOUNDS:
    impractical __ : __ : __ : __ : __ : __ : __ practical*

THE SPEAKER IS A:
    poor learner __ : __ : __ : __ : __ : __ : __ good learner*

THE SPEAKER SOUNDS:
    incoherent __ : __ : __ : __ : __ : __ : __ coherent*

THE SPEAKER SOUNDS:
    *decisive __ : __ : __ : __ : __ : __ : __ indecisive

THE SPEAKER SOUNDS:
    unintelligent __ : __ : __ : __ : __ : __ : __ intelligent*

TABLE 6.5 (continued)

THE SPEAKER SOUNDS:
  unfriendly __ : __ : __ : __ : __ : __ : __ friendly*

THE SPEAKER SOUNDS:
  timid __ : __ : __ : __ : __ : __ : __ self-assured*

THE SPEAKER SOUNDS:
  disagreeable __ : __ : __ : __ : __ : __ : __ agreeable*

THE SPEAKER SOUNDS:
  unsure of himself __ : __ : __ : __ : __ : __ : __ sure of himself*

---

*The asterisks define the pole of the scale assigned a value of 1.0 in the quantification scheme; the asterisks did not appear on the actual instrument.

Results. Factor analysis of the 40 attitude scales revealed four factors composed of 19 scales. When those scales which loaded lower than .60 were eliminated, a four-factor, 15-scale instrument remained (Table 6.6). Factor I appeared to be concerned with the speaker's INTELLIGENCE and COMPETENCE to do a job and accounted for 26.4% of the variance. Factor II, composed of four scales, measured perception of the speaker's AGREEABLENESS and accounted for 16.3% of the variance. Factor III appeared to measure perception of the speaker's SELF-ASSURANCE and accounted for 16.5% of the variance. Factor IV was comprised of the single scale ANGLO-LIKE–NON-ANGLO-LIKE and accounted for 7.5% of the variance. It was decided to include this scale in subsequent analysis in order to replicate the rather surprising finding that ethnicity seemed to exert little influence either upon speech attitudes or hiring decisions.

Factor analysis of the seven job scales revealed a two-factor structure (Table 6.7). Factor 1 (44.93% variance) was composed of the five scales PUBLIC RELATIONS, EXECUTIVE, FOREMAN, SALES, and MANUAL LABOR, the last of which loaded negatively. Factor 2 was composed of the scales CLERICAL and SKILLED TECHNICIAN and accounted for 23.34% of the variance.

Regression analyses were then conducted using standardized job factor scores as criterion variables and the standardized attitude factor scores as predictor variables. Separate analyses were also run using the individual job scales scores as criterion variables. The results of these analyses are summarized in Table 6.8.

TABLE 6.6
*Rotated Factor Matrix of Employers' Responses
to Stimuli (Phase I)*

Variables	Factors			
	I	II	III	IV
1. Eager	.67*	.27	.09	.06
2. Cooperative	.28	.71*	-.13	.08
3. Agreeable	.08	.81*	.06	-.01
4. Self-assured	.28	.03	.73*	-.03
5. Relaxed	.12	.07	.84	.14
6. Expresses self well	.67*	.15	.54	-.10
7. Organized	.76*	.08	.36	.09
8. Thorough	.66*	.30	.26	-.23
9. Warm	.07	.66*	.41	-.23
10. Straightforward	.68*	.23	.34	.00
11. Intelligent	.79*	.13	.07	-.01
12. Dependable	.24	.72*	.16	.11
13. Concise	.75*	.14	.09	.16
14. Calm	.37	.02	.60*	.28
15. Anglo-like	.04	.02	.14	.89*
% total variance	26.4	16.3	16.5	7.5

*Items loading highest on factor indicated.

The highest predictive capability for the four factors was obtained with composite job Factor 1, which involved basically white-collar types of jobs.

Analysis of job Factor 2 and the individual hiring decision scales indicate that an employer's perception of speech characteristics has greater predictive value when the decision is being made relative to a white-collar or supervisory type of position than when it is relative to a clerical or technical position.

These findings indicate that employers seem to make judgments about the intelligence and competence of a person to do a job, his self-assurance, his agreeability, and his ethnicity. Further it seems likely that knowledge of these judgments are of value in predicting the employment decision. The employment decision appears to be based primarily upon employer perception of the

TABLE 6.7

Rotated Factor Matrix of Employers' Hiring Decisions (Phase I)

Variable	Factors	
	1	2
1. Skilled Technician	.24	.86*
2. Clerical	-.11	.88*
3. Manual Labor	-.56*	.21
4. Public Relations	.88*	.01
5. Executive	.86*	.05
6. Foreman	.79*	.17
7. Sales	.79*	.19
% total variance	45	23

*Items loading highest on factor indicated.

TABLE 6.8

Prediction of Hiring Decisions from Four Attitude Factors (Phase I)

Job Category	R	R^2	Relative contributions of factors			
			I*	II	III	IV
Clerical	.43**	.18	.12	.02	.03	.01
Skilled Technician	.34**	.11	.03	.03	.00	.04
Manual Labor	.40**	.16	.13	.00	.02	.01
Public Relations	.59**	.35	.26	.01	.08	.00
Executive	.56**	.31	.13	.04	.14	.00
Foreman	.65**	.42	.33	.00	.07	.02
Sales	.60**	.36	.23	.01	.11	.01
Composite Factor 1	.68**	.47	.33	.01	.13	.00
Composite Factor 2	.36**	.13	.05	.03	.00	.03

*Attitude factors.　　　　　　　　　　　　　**$p < .01$ for $d.f.$ 3,88

　I = Intelligence–Competence　　　　　II = Agreeable–Dependable
III = Relaxed–Self-assured　　　　　　IV = Anglo-like–Non-Anglo-like

speaker's ability to perform a job and to a lesser extent on perception of his confidence. Relatively little emphasis is placed on the degree to which the potential employee is perceived to be agreeable and dependable and still less on the degree to which he is perceived to be Anglo-like. Also, it was of interest to note that judgments of ethnicity appeared to have had little relation to the employment decision. The researchers speculate that recent Federal legislation designed to eliminate the effects of ethnicity on employability may actually be having the desired effect on employers. Many of the employers interviewed appeared to be sensitive to the necessity of making available jobs to members of minority groups, and many indicated strongly that their establishments were making energetic efforts to assure fair treatment of such people. The results indicate that the main concern of these employers was whether the interviewee was capable of performing the task to which he was assigned. Such considerations, along with a desire for replication and validation of the test instrument, led directly to the second study.

Study II: Scale Application

Method. Utilizing the 14-scale instrument developed earlier, field workers presented forty employers from the same Austin list with taped samples of persons answering questions typical of the employment interview. Speakers for this study included two Blacks, one White "deep South" speaker, and one standard English speaker. Employers again listened to 90-second samples of each speaker, rated the speech, as well as the probability that he would hire him for each of five job categories.

Results. Factor analysis of the attitude scales revealed a factor structure almost identical to that found earlier (Table 6.9). Three factors accounted for 67% of the variance in the model. Factor I consisted of the five scales organized—disorganized, concise—repetitive, intelligent—unintelligent, straightforward—evasive, and thorough—superficial, accounting for 28% of the variance; this factor seemed to represent a judgment of the speaker's overall competence to perform a job. Factor II consisted of the scales agreeable—disagreeable, cooperative—uncooperative, and warm—cold, and accounted for 18% of the variance. Factor III accounted for 21% of the variance, and the three scales relaxed—tense, calm—frightened, and self-assured—timid all loaded negatively on the factor. All eleven of these scales loaded higher than .65 with the three factors.

On the basis of the factor analyses conducted in the two studies, it was concluded that employers make stable judgments of the speech characteristics of persons being interviewed for employment. These judgments appear to be

TABLE 6.9

Rotated Factor Matrix of Employer's Responses
to Stimuli (Phase II)

	Factors		
Variables	I	II	III
1. Organized	.81*	.09	-.20
2. Calm	.22	.27	-.83*
3. Warm	.08	.71*	-.25
4. Thorough	.68*	.30	-.10
5. Concise	.77*	.05	-.21
6. Cooperative	.10	.79*	-.20
7. Agreeable	.28	.80*	.00
8. Intelligent	.74*	.22	-.07
9. Relaxed	.17	.11	-.86*
10. Straightforward	.69*	.05	-.30
11. Self-assured	.35	.14	-.76*
% total variance	28	18	21

*Items loading highest on factor indicated.

concerned with whether an applicant is COMPETENT, AGREEABLE, and SELF-ASSURED.

Factor analysis of the five employability scales revealed two factors (Table 6.10). Factor 1 consisted of the scales "executive, foreman," and "skilled technician," while Factor 2 was comprised of the scales "clerical" and "manual." This represented a change from the first study where "manual" had loaded negatively on Factor 1 and "skilled technician" had loaded with "clerical occupations." This led to the conclusion that employers' groupings of job categories might not be as stable as their judgments of speech characteristics.

Standardized factor scores for the two employability factors and the three speech rating factors were obtained, and regression analyses were conducted using as predictors the attitude factor scores and the employability ratings on each of the two factors as criterion variables. Equation 1 (Table 6.11) revealed an $R = .54$ for the three attitude factors of Factor 1 of the employability scales,

TABLE 6.10

Rotated Factor Matrix of Employers' Hiring
Decision (Phase II)

	Factors	
Variable	1	2
1. Executive	.85*	-.03
2. Foreman	.86*	.13
3. Skilled Technician	.74*	.35
4. Manual labor	-.12	.85*
5. Clerical	.07	.55*
% total variance	.42	.26

*Items loading highest on factor indicated.

indicating that the attitude factors explained 29% of the variance in the criterion variable. Equation 2, using job Factor 2 as the criterion, revealed no significant correlations between speech ratings and employment decisions.

Due to the instability of the employability factors, separate regression analyses were conducted using each of the five employability scales as criterion variables. The results of these analyses (both by individual scales and composite employment-decision factors) also appear in Table 6.11. The results indicate that employer ratings of speech characteristics are fair predictors of employability for the executive or leadership job categories but have no predictive value for the manual category. While the relative contributions on the five job scales make sense, and four of the models yield R's significantly greater than zero, the findings in Study I represent a drop in predictive value from those of Study II.

A discriminant analysis (Table 6.12) of the hiring decisions for each of the four speakers revealed significant differences only for the executive job category. The standard English speaker was rated as being the most employable. For the category of foreman, the difference approached significance with the standard English speaker again being the most favored. For those positions perceived as being of a less white-collar or supervisory nature, differences among judgments of the four speakers were nonsignificant. This analysis confirms the judgment that speech characteristics have greater predictive value when the application is for a white-collar type of position and that employers will tend to favor standard English speakers for those positions.

TABLE 6.11
Prediction of Hiring Decisions from Three Attitude Factors (Phase II)

Model No.	Job Category	$\underline{R}$	$\underline{R}^2$	Relative Contribution		
				Intelligent-Competent	Agreeable-Dependable	Relaxed-Self-assured
3	Executive	.38**	.14	.13	.01	.00
4	Foreman	.38**	.14	.14	.00	.00
5	Skilled Technician	.36**	.13	.12	.01	.00
6	Manual Labor	.18	.03	.02	.00	.01
7	Clerical	.28**	.08	.05	.00	.05
1	Composite Factor 1 (Ex., Foreman, Sk. T.)	.54**	.29	.26	.03	.00
2	Composite Factor 2 (Clerical, Manual)	.17	.03	.01	.00	.02

**p < .01 for d.f. 2,157

TABLE 6.12
Discriminant Analysis of 4 Speakers by Hiring Decisions

Variable	Group mean				p
	I	II	III	IV	
Executive	3.65	3.45	3.82	2.87*	.002
Foreman	3.10	2.92	3.45	2.87	.07
Skilled Technician	2.82	2.92	2.75	2.42	.17
Manual Labor	3.20	3.54	3.05	3.32	.26
Clerical	3.00	4.30	4.10	4.60	.17

*Low score indicates a greater probability of employment.

I = Black speaker #1
II = Black speaker #2
III = White ethnic speaker
IV = Standard English speaker

Discussion

The major finding of this project was in the stability of employers' attitude judgments. The three-factor structure (INTELLIGENT-COMPETENT, SELF-ASSURED, AGREEABLE) of employer judgments was replicated across 62 employers and two sets of stimulus materials.

Only the first of these factors, INTELLIGENT-COMPETENT, served as a consistent predictor of employment decisions. Its predictability was strongest in distinctly higher-status occupations. Added to this was the discriminant analysis which showed significant differences among speakers only for the executive job decision. This suggests that employee speech characteristics and the employer attitudes which they stimulate are important predictors in success of job interviews for executive and supervisory positions. This is reasonable, since the work in such positions is highly speech-related.

By contrast, speech seems less important as a predictor of success in job interviews for manual labor positions. This is again intuitively reasonable, since speaking the standard dialect may be less effective in such positions. Between these extremes lie the categories of foreman, clerical, and technical positions. Speech appears to be a partial predictor of success in these interviews but perhaps not a vital one.

Subsequent research may clear up some of the questions raised in Study II. It is possible that the inclusion of a second Black speaker may have reduced variation in the employability scales somewhat. Study II tapes were also judged less content-free than the Study I tapes, and there were two interviewers asking speakers the questions, which may have induced unaccounted for variance.

The present research suggests several lines of further research. First, it would be informative to use larger numbers of speaker tapes, in which there were representative samples of ethnic groups, both sexes, all social class groupings, and ages. Second, it would be interesting to analyze employer ratings using Q-analysis techniques to ascertain "kinds of employer-interviewers," in terms of how they make hiring decisions. Finally, it would be informative to manipulate the speech samples in terms of particular linguistic or usage aspects of speech, to see if such particular variations affected employment decisions. It is anticipated that such tapes could be made by linguistic informants capable of code-switching. It would also be interesting to provide employers with additional information about the speakers, either by using videotapes or by using written vita sheets (to add a dimension of qualifications, experience).

Some Closing Notes

Most of the immediate implications or theoretical interpretations and suggestions for research have already been incorporated in many places throughout the preceding chapters. As a consequence, our closing notes on the monograph will focus only upon several issues that we feel have not been emphasized already.

Generality

One important point in considering the studies as a whole is the degree of confidence that we have in the generality of the two-factor judgmental model. Although it seems to apply consistently across child and teacher types, the particular ratings that a child receives are probably highly tied to the nature of the speech situation. Reflecting upon this, we must admit to a highly restricted sampling of speech situations in this research. In almost all cases, the child's speech represented a language style that he might bring to bear when a moderate degree of standard English is expected in a semi-formal situation. In the Chicago study, this was conversation with a linguistic field worker; in the Texas studies, this was conversation with a person presented to them as a teacher. In short, almost all the measures throughout this monograph are restricted to one particular speech style of the children. Obviously, if speech samples were drawn from peer situations, for example, we might expect the same children to be rated differently on the two dimensions. To reiterate the point: the model, we think, has generality, but the ratings of a given child may vary substantially. One intriguing question is whether "latitude of acceptance" reflects this anticipated variation.

Research Strategy

If it has not been clear thus far, it could be stated explicitly that the overall strategy used in most of the present projects is amenable to many further areas of investigation of types of speakers, speech situations, and listeners. That is, if we are interested in linguistic attitudes in some particular situation where we may sample populations of speakers, speech and listeners, it is possible to employ the overall strategy of:

(1) sampling representative language samples from that situation,
(2) eliciting free discussion from representatives of the listener population in response to those language samples,
(3) developing prototype semantic differential instruments and gaining pilot data in ratings of speech samples,
(4) analyzing listeners' use of the scales to determine if there are basic dimensions of evaluation, and
(5) applying a refined instrument in the analysis of varieties of speech found in that particular situation.

Changing Attitudes

There is no reason why manipulations of linguistic attitude could not be pursued with the strategies found in social psychological experiments in attitude change. If undertaken, the present two-factor model would be a way of gauging effects.

Theoretical Inquiry

A final suggestion, and hopefully the greatest challenge, is to pursue theoretical questions about how the attitudinal processes apply to language. In several points in this monograph, we have loosely speculated on how a judgmental process may work. Again, in a judgmental situation this process may follow such steps as:

(1) persons' initial attitudes are stimulated with any cue that will elicit a stereotype,
(2) the stereotype then serves in mediating attitudes toward the particular stimulus being evaluated, and
(3) whatever final judgment is made about a child represents a combination of stereotype characteristics of the child and a person's range of acceptability of linguistic attitudes.

Obviously, the lines of further research are nearly unlimited.

references

Anisfeld, M., & Lambert, W. E. Evaluational reactions of bilingual and monolingual children to spoken languages. *Journal of Abnormal and Social Psychology,* 1964, 69, 89-97.

Anisfeld, M., Bogo, N., & Lambert, W. E. Evaluational reactions to accented English speech. *Journal of Abnormal and Social Psychology,* 1962, 65, 223-31.

Baird, S. J. Employment interview speech: A social dialect study in Austin, Texas. Unpublished doctoral dissertation, University of Texas, 1969.

Bouchard-Ryan, E. L. Psycholinguistic attitude study. *Studies in Language and Language Behavior, Progress Report No. VII.* Center for Research on Language and Language Behavior, The University of Michigan, February 1, 1969.

Bourhis, R. Y., Giles, H., & Lambert, W. E. Social consequences of accommodating one's style of speech: A cross-national investigation. Unpublished manuscript, July 1972.

Buck, J. The effects of Negro and White dialectical variations upon attitudes of college students. *Speech Monographs,* 1968, 35, 181-86.

Cheyne, W. M. Stereotyped reactions to speakers with Scottish and English regional accents. *British Journal of Social and Clinical Psychology,* 1970, 9, 77-79.

d'Anglejan, A. & Tucker, G. R. Sociolinguistic correlates of speech style in Quebec. Unpublished manuscript, McGill University, undated.

Darlington, R. B. Multiple regression in psychological research and practice. *Psychological Bulletin,* 1968, 79, 161-82.

Duncan, D. B. Multiple range and multiple F tests. *Biometrics,* 1955, 11, 1-42.

Findley, C. A. Social acceptability and employability: An experimental study of the effects of structural maturity and four grammatical features on judgments of employability. Ann Arbor, Mich.: University Microfilms, August 1971.

Fleming, E. S., & Anttonen, R. G. Teacher expectancy or 'My Fair Lady.' *American Educational Research Journal,* 1971, 8, 241-52.

Fraser, B. Some 'unexpected' reactions to various American-English dialects. Unpublished manuscript, Language Research Foundation, 1972.

Frender, R., & Lambert, W. E. The influence of pupils' speech styles on teacher evaluations. Paper presented at the 23rd Annual Round Table Meeting, Georgetown University, Washington, D. C., 1972.

Giles, H. Patterns of evaluation to R. P., South Welsh and Somerset accented speech. *British Journal of Social and Clinical Psychology,* 1971, 10, 280-81.

Guilford, J. P. *Fundamental statistics in psychology and education.* New York: McGraw-Hill, 1956.

Guskin, J. T. The social perception of language variation: Black and White teachers' attitudes towards speakers from different racial and social class backgrounds. Unpublished doctoral dissertation, #10,056, The University of Michigan, 1970.

Harms, L. S. Listener judgments of status cues in speech. *Quarterly Journal of Speech,* 1961, 47, 164-68.

———. Status cues in speech: Extra-race and extra-region identification. *Lingua,* 1963, 12, 300-306.

Hewett, N. Reactions of prospective English teachers toward speakers of a nonstandard dialect. *Language Learning,* 1971, 21, 205-12.

Hollingshead, A. B. *Two-factor index of social position.* New Haven: by the Author, Yale Station, New Haven, Connecticut (c. 1957 as *Two-factor index of status position*), 1965.

Hollingshead, A. B., & Redlich, F. C. *Social class and mental illness.* New York: John Wiley, 1958.

Hopper, R., Hewett, N., Smith, D. B., & Watkins, C. Speech characteristics and employability. *Communication Research Notes:* an occasional publication of the Center for Communication Research, School of Communication, University of Texas at Austin, Austin, Texas, 1972.

Hopper, R., & Williams, F. Speech characteristics and employability. *Speech Monographs,* 1973, 40, 296-302.

Labov, W. *The social stratification of English in New York City.* Washington, D. C.: Center for Applied Linguistics, 1966.

Lambert, W. E. Psychological approaches to the study of language, part II: On second language learning and bilingualism. *The Modern Language Journal,* 1963, 47, 114-21.

———. A social psychology of bilingualism. *The Journal of Social Issues,* 1967, 23, 91-109.

Lambert, W. E., Anisfeld, M., & Yeni-Komshian, G. Evaluational reactions of Jewish and Arab adolescents to dialect and language variations. *Journal of Personality and Social Psychology,* 1965, 2, 84-90.

Lambert, W. E., Frankel, H., & Tucker, G. R. Judging personality through speech: A French-Canadian example. *Journal of Communication,* 1966, 16, 305-21.

Lambert, W. E., Hodgson, R. C., Gardner, R. C., & Fillenbaum, S. Evaluational reactions to spoken languages. *Journal of Abnormal Social Psychology,* 1960, 60, 44-51.

Maclay, H., & Osgood, C. E. Hesitation phenomena in spontaneous English speech. *Word* 1959, 15, 19-44.

Miller, L. M. Evaluational reactions of Mexican-American and Anglo teachers to children's speech. *Western Speech,* 1972, 36, 109-14.

Moe, J. D. Listener judgments of status cues in speech: A replication and extension. *Speech Monographs,* 1972, 39, 144-47.

Mortensen, C. D., & Sereno, K. K. The influence of ego-involvement and discrepancy on perceptions of communication. *Speech Monographs,* 1970, 37, 127-34.

Naremore, R. C. Teachers' judgments of children's speech: A factor analytic study of attitudes. *Speech Monographs,* 1971, 38, 17-27.

Osgood, C. E. Studies on the generality of affective meaning systems. *American Psychologist,* 1962, 17, 10-28.

———. Semantic differential technique in the comparative study of cultures. *American Anthropologist,* 1964, 66, 171-200.

Osgood, C. E., Suci, G. J., & Tannenbaum, P. H. *The measurement of meaning.* Urbana: University of Illinois Press, 1957.

Perkins, H. A. Teacher reaction to children speaking standard or nonstandard English: Notes on the experiment and the results. Unpublished manuscript from UCLA, TESL, M. A. Colloquium, January 1971.

Preston, M. S. Evaluational reactions to English, Canadian French, and European French voices. Unpublished master's thesis, McGill University, 1963.

Putnam, G. N., & O'Hern, E. The status significance of an isolated urban dialect. *Language,* 1955, 31, 1-32.

Rokeach, M. *The open and closed mind.* New York: Basic Books, 1960.

Rosenthal, R., & Jacobson, L. *Pygmalion in the classroom.* New York: Holt, Rinehart, and Winston, 1968.

Rosenthal, R., & Jacobson, L. F. Teacher expectations for the disadvantaged. *Scientific American,* 1968, 218, 19-23.

Seligman, C. R., Tucker, G. R., & Lambert, W. E. The effects of speech style and other attributes on teachers' attitudes toward pupils. *Language in Society,* 1972, I, 131-42.

Sherif, C. W., Sherif, M., & Nebergall, R. E. *Attitude and attitude change.* Philadelphia: W. B. Saunders Company, 1965.

Shuy, R. W. Detroit speech: Careless, awkward, and inconsistent, or systematic, graceful, and regular? *Elementary English,* 1968, 45, 565-69.

———. Employee selection, training, promotion: Pitfalls of good intentions. A prepublication version of a paper presented at the C.A.L.-N.C.T.E. Conference, Education and Training in the National Interest: The Role of Language Variety, February 13-14, 1970.

Shuy, R. W., Baratz, J. C., & Wolfram, W. A. *Sociolinguistic factors in speech identification.* National Institute of Mental Health Research Project No. MH-15048-01, Center for Applied Linguistics, 1969.

Shuy, R. W., Wolfram, W. A., & Riley, W. K. Linguistic correlates of social stratification in Detroit speech. Cooperative Research Project No. 6-1347, Michigan State University, mimeo, 1967.

Stephenson, W. *The study of behavior: Q-technique and its methodology.* Chicago: University of Chicago Press, 1953.

Strongman, K. T., & Woosley, J. Stereotyped reactions to regional accents. *British Journal of Social and Clinical Psychology,* 1967, 6, 164-67.

Tucker, G. R., & Lambert, W. E. White and Negro listeners' reactions to various American-English dialects. *Social Forces,* 1969, 47, 463-68.

Whitehead, J. L., & Miller, L. Correspondence between evaluations of children's speech and speech anticipated upon the basis of stereotype. *Southern Speech Communications Journal,* 1972, 37, 375-86.

Williams, F. *Language and poverty: Perspectives on a theme.* Institute for Research on Poverty Monograph Series. Chicago: Markham, 1970(a).

———. Psychological correlates of speech characteristics: On sounding "disadvantaged." *Journal of Speech and Hearing Research,* 1970(b), 13, 472-88.

Williams, F., & Miller, L. M. Effects of dialect switching on language and personality evaluations. Unpublished manuscript, December 1971.

Williams, F., & Naremore, R. C. On the functional analysis of social class differences in models of speech. *Speech Monographs,* 1969(a), 36, 77-102.

———. Social class differences in children's syntactic performance: A quantitative analysis of field study data. *Journal of Speech and Hearing Research,* 1969(b), 12, 777-93.

———. Language attitudes: A follow-up analysis of teacher differences. *Speech Monographs,* 1974, 41, 391-396.

Williams, F., & Shamo, G. W. Regional variations in teacher attitudes toward children's language. *Central States Speech Journal,* 1972, 23, 73-77.

Williams, F., Whitehead, J. L., & Miller, L. M. *Attitudinal correlates of children's speech characteristics.* Final Report Project No. 0-0336, Grant No. OEG-0-70-7868 (508), U. S. Department of Health, Education, and Welfare. Office of Education, Bureau of Research, March 1971(a).

———. Ethnic stereotyping and judgments of children's speech. *Speech Monographs,* 1971(b), 38, 166-70.

Williams, F., Whitehead, J. L., & Miller, L. Relations between language attitudes and teacher expectancy. *American Educational Research Journal,* 1972, 9, 263-77.

Wölck, W. Attitudes toward Spanish and Quechua in bilingual Peru. Manuscript prepared for the session on Social and Ethnic Diversity: Subjective Reactions to Language, 23rd Georgetown Round Table Meeting, Washington, D. C., March 16, 1972.